HBR Guide to
Better Recruiting and Hiring

Harvard Business Review Guides

Arm yourself with the advice you need to succeed on the job, from the most trusted brand in business. Packed with how-to essentials from leading experts, the HBR Guides provide smart answers to your most pressing work challenges.

The titles include:

HBR Guide for Women at Work

HBR Guide to AI Basics for Managers

HBR Guide to Being a Great Boss

HBR Guide to Being More Productive

HBR Guide to Better Business Writing

HBR Guide to Better Mental Health at Work

HBR Guide to Better Recruiting and Hiring

HBR Guide to Building Your Business Case

HBR Guide to Buying a Small Business

HBR Guide to Changing Your Career

HBR Guide to Coaching Employees

HBR Guide to Collaborative Teams

HBR Guide to Critical Thinking

HBR Guide to Data Analytics Basics for Managers

HBR Guide to Dealing with Conflict

HBR Guide to Delivering Effective Feedback

HBR Guide to Designing Your Retirement

HBR Guide to Emotional Intelligence

HBR Guide to
Better Recruiting and Hiring

HARVARD BUSINESS REVIEW PRESS

Boston, Massachusetts

Copyright 2025 Harvard Business School Publishing Corporation

Printed in the United States of America

10 9 8 7 6 5 4 3 2

The web addresses referenced in this book were live and correct at the time of the book's publication but may be subject to change.

Library of Congress Cataloging-in-Publication Data

Title: HBR guide to better recruiting and hiring / Harvard Business Review.
Other titles: Harvard Business Review guide to better recruiting and hiring
Description: Boston, Massachusetts : Harvard Business Review Press, [2025]
   | Series: HBR guides | Includes index. |
Identifiers: LCCN 2024032817 (print) | LCCN 2024032818 (ebook) | ISBN
   9798892790000 (paperback) | ISBN 9798892790017 (epub)
Subjects: LCSH: Employees—Recruiting | Employee selection.
Classification: LCC HF5549.5.R44 H37 2025 (print) | LCC HF5549.5.R44
   (ebook) | DDC 658.3/11—dc23/eng/20240828
LC record available at https://lccn.loc.gov/2024032817
LC ebook record available at https://lccn.loc.gov/2024032818

ISBN: 979-8-89279-000-0
eISBN: 979-8-89279-001-7

The paper used in this publication meets the requirements of the American National Standard for Permanence of Paper for Publications and Documents in Libraries and Archives Z39.48-1992.

What You'll Learn

Filling an open position is an opportunity—and a challenge. Whether you're replacing someone or you've successfully lobbied to add headcount, this is your chance to add new skills and abilities—and a great teammate—to your organization. As a manager, when you're recruiting and hiring, you need to reflect and prepare just as much as the candidates do. While it may be tempting to recycle an existing job description (or create one featuring an unattainable wish list of skills) you should think critically about what will serve your team now and in the years to come. Making a bad hire can reverberate widely, with high costs to your team and to people's faith in you. Making a good hire can boost your confidence, build trust with your colleagues, and even elevate your leadership presence.

You want to attract, identify, and hire people whose values, competencies, and potential align with your team and your organization. Where can you find new sources of talent? What's the best way to ascertain both what candidates are ready to do on day one and how they might be able to learn and grow? What hiring process will allow more candidates to be more fully themselves? How can you make data-driven decisions that reduce bias? What steps can you take to keep people engaged in a process that may swing from painfully slow to uncomfortably fast? How can you be sure you're thinking critically about not only what this role has meant in the past but also how it could transform in the future?

This guide will help you:

- Assess your team's strengths and weaknesses

- Identify the attributes and qualifications you need

- Craft a compelling and accurate job description

- Increase the size and quality of the candidate pool

- Build a strong partnership with HR

- Reduce personal bias in hiring practices

- Conduct effective interviews

- Assess cultural fit—and future performance

- Get people excited about the role and your company

- Make a fair and competitive offer

- Negotiate with confidence

Contents

Contents

SECTION TWO

Attract and Build a Wide Pool of Candidates

SECTION THREE

Conduct Effective Interviews

Contents

SECTION SIX

Make an Offer or Reject Candidates

Contents

HBR Guide to
**Better Recruiting
and Hiring**

Managers Are the Keys to the Future of Work—and the Hiring Process

by Emily Field and Bryan Hancock

Making great hires for your organization requires strategy. Larry, a manager we interviewed for our book *Power to the Middle,* has embraced his role as a hiring manager to help his company better compete in a challenging labor market. Instead of relying on salary to attract and retain workers, he emphasizes what his company offers in alignment with what candidates seek: growth opportunities, individual purpose, and company culture.

As Larry has learned, the hiring manager role is critical—and often all-consuming. It requires duties, tasks, and relationships that might not always be part of your day-to-day job. You must keep your team on track while also serving as the "face" and "voice" of the company—perhaps even candidates' first experience of your organization. You serve as the primary conduit to deliver the perspective on value and purpose that prospective employees seek, not only to attract more top-level talent but also to keep them around. You're responsible for communicating what working at the company will be like.

And that message is important to get right, since employees are increasingly seeking human connection and purpose through their daily work. A recent survey found that 51% those who left their job within a six-month period lacked a sense of belonging at work.[1] Thirty-one percent of those who left their job between April 2021 and April 2022 cited lack of meaningful work as a reason.[2]

With more than enough on your plate—planning, reporting, and approval tasks that accumulate into a mountain of work—it may be tempting to hand off the recruitment, assessment, and hiring of candidates to HR. After all, your goal is to free up more time to lead and coach your teams, and, as we have shared in *Power to the Middle,* McKinsey research finds that managers already spend nearly half of their time (49%) handling nonmanagerial work, such as administrative and individual-contributor tasks.[3] It's not surprising, then, that more than a third of managers (35%) say they don't have the resources required to make talent and people management a priority.[4] The *HBR Guide to Better Recruiting and Hiring* can help; it provides the tips, insights, and basic foundation you'll need to navigate the hiring process more efficiently and thoughtfully.

An open position on your team is an opportunity to reimagine your role as manager: You are a driver of talent acquisition, and you are helping guide your organization's talent strategy. In partnership with HR, you are in the position to help your organization explore new sources of talent, bring in much-needed skills and new perspectives, and ultimately shape the workforce for the future.

Hiring managers also need to consider the role that AI can play in the hiring process. This guide will help you understand where it's best applied—and where it's not. Technology can and should be used throughout the process to strengthen you as a hiring manager; for instance, it can help you develop job descriptions based on necessary skills, reduce bias in evaluating candidates, and communicate more effectively with all participants throughout the process. But it can't replace you in this role. The final call about whom to hire remains a decision for you and your hiring team to make.

Finding and fostering talent is perhaps your most important role within your organization. To get—and keep—the talent you need requires invested time and effort, in partnership with HR. The *HBR Guide to Better Recruiting and Hiring* includes resources to help you attract, assess, and decide on the candidate who will move your team forward. You are a key player in helping your company win in today's fierce competition for talent, and this book will be your guide.

What This Book Will Do

This curated collection of articles is for individual managers—not organizations, HR, or professional recruiters. It's for anyone, at any age or career stage, who leads a team, unit, or division and manages other people. Whether you are an experienced hiring manager, new to the process, or somewhere in between, this book will help you effectively partner with HR and your team to better attract, recruit, and hire candidates who are the best fit for what you're seeking.

The experts in this collection will increase your understanding of the big-picture hiring process, including how you think about open positions and what candidates may bring to them. It will address many of the challenges and opportunities that this process presents, and it will help you build the skills you need to find and hire people whose values, competencies, and potential best align with your team and organization.

What's Ahead

The process of attracting, hiring, and retaining great employees is not easy, and there's no perfect way to define the "ideal" candidate for any role. There are many factors to consider, from current skill sets, to background, to capacity to learn and grow, to anticipating what you'll need in an ever-evolving context.

Additionally, candidates may not always be truthful or forthright, interview teams may not always agree, the pace may move slower or faster than you'd prefer, biases may be introduced, and your top choice may turn down your offer.

But as a manager, you are uniquely positioned to help your team and organization grow by strategically adding new perspectives, skills, and expertise. You can lean into new sources of talent. You can drive the hiring process by thinking critically about what needs to be done and who can best complement the collective team. You can start to shape the employee experience from the beginning so that great hires are more likely to stick around. This guide can help you do just that.

––––––––––––

Emily Field is a partner in McKinsey's Seattle office. She works with leaders to shape data-driven organizational strategies designed to achieve business objectives, establish talent management as a distinctive advantage, and secure the human resources function as a driver of business value.

Bryan Hancock is a partner in McKinsey's Washington, DC, office and the global leader of McKinsey's talent work. He has served a wide range of talent-intensive businesses, leading employers in sectors such as retail, transportation, logistics, health care, banking, asset management, and oil and gas.

Both are authors of the book *Power to the Middle*, which argues for a profound reimagining of what middle managers, the true center of the organization, can and must do.

NOTES

1. Aaron De Smet, Bonnie Dowling, Marino Mugayar-Baldocchi, and Joe Spratt, "It's Not About the Office, It's About Belonging," mckinsey.com, January 13, 2022, https://www.mckinsey.com/capabilities/people-and-organizational-performance/our-insights/the-organization-blog/its-not-about-the-office-its-about-belonging.

2. Aaron De Smet, Bonnie Dowling, Bryan Hancock, and Bill Schaninger, "The Great Attrition Is Making Hiring Harder. Are You Searching the Right Talent Pools?," *McKinsey Quarterly*, July 13, 2022, https://www.mckinsey.com/capabilities/people-and-organizational-performance/our-insights/the-great-attrition-is-making-hiring-harder-are-you-searching-the-right-talent-pools.

3. Emily Field, Bryan Hancock, Marino Mugayar-Baldocchi, and Bill Schaninger, "Stop Wasting Your Most Precious Resource: Middle Managers," mckinsey.com, March 10, 2023, https://www.mckinsey.com/capabilities/people-and-organizational-performance/our-insights/stop-wasting-your-most-precious-resource-middle-managers.

4. Field, Hancock, Mugayar-Baldocchi, and Schaninger, "Stop Wasting Your Most Precious Resource: Middle Managers," mckinsey.com, March 10, 2023, https://www.mckinsey.com/capabilities/people-and-organizational-performance/our-insights/stop-wasting-your-most-precious-resource-middle-managers.

Understand the Process

SECTION ONE

Understand the
process

CHAPTER 1

How to Hire Top Talent

by Ryan Renteria

All managers need a few essential skills to successfully lead and make an impact in their organization. Communication, decision-making, empathy, and adaptability are some of the capabilities most widely researched and written about in the business world. There is one skill, however, that's often less discussed—learning how to hire top talent.

In my 22 years of experience on Wall Street, in professional sports, and most recently as an executive coach, I've seen the positive impact a great hiring strategy can have on a manager's career. While you may not always

---

Adapted from "New Leaders, Here's How to Hire a Top Talent" on hbr.org, January 2, 2024.

have the power to choose your team, learning how to spot and appeal to high-performing candidates can fundamentally impact your trajectory.

What do I mean by top talent? Stellar hard skills—the technical skills needed to perform a specific role—are table stakes. You should also be looking for a few vital soft skills:

- **Intrinsic motivation:** Top talent means people who are motivated by their own desire to learn and grow. Their behavior or past experiences demonstrate curiosity, autonomy, and resourcefulness in solving problems or overcoming challenging work situations.

- **Perseverance:** A top job candidate should display open-mindedness and adaptability. These are people who've shown they can navigate uncertainty and unexpected roadblocks.

- **Reliability:** Top talent are reliable—people with strong organizational skills who pay attention to detail. They meet deadlines. You can trust them to get things right and deliver quality work.

A team of people who possess these qualities can be trusted to execute tasks on time and to a high standard. This allows you to delegate tasks and assign projects that are relevant to their individual areas of expertise. This creates a win-win situation for everyone. It gives your direct reports more opportunities to take on visible work that will help them grow and potentially introduce them to powerful stakeholders throughout the company.

It also creates space for you to engage in bigger-picture, strategic thinking about your organization's business goals and how your team can help them come to fruition. You'll have more time to develop strategic team goals, improve on processes that may be slowing you down, and produce results.

Moreover, a strong and reliable team creates fewer fires for you to put out. This leaves you less susceptible to the burnout that harms leadership careers, personal lives, and mental health.

Whether you're new to hiring or looking for a quick refresher because it's been a while since you've sat on this side of the table, here are the most important steps to increase your odds of making a great hire.

Develop a Strong Hiring Process

I once worked with a client who had a meticulous hiring process and a reliable team; that is, until Brad (not his real name) joined the company. One of my client's team members—let's call him Christopher—slipped up during the interview process. When Christopher interviewed Brad, he fell in love with his background and qualifications. Worried that another company would snatch him up, Christopher offered Brad the job just a few days after the person he was replacing announced his retirement. In the end, Brad struggled to meet the expectations of the role. Because he wasn't thoroughly vetted, neither Brad nor the company were set up for success.

You can avoid critical mistakes like Christopher's by mastering three parts of a hiring process:

1. Write a strong job description

The first step to landing a talented candidate is to sell them with an incredible first impression. This starts with the job description. If you're able to weigh in on this aspect of the application, ask yourself the following questions: Why would your company be the right one for your ideal candidate? How is your company different from the other options it may be considering?

In the description itself, focus on the following areas:

Start by describing your company's purpose

What are you trying to achieve in the marketplace? Why should anyone care? How is your culture different from others out there? A good match for the role should read the job description and think, "Wow, this company really aligns with my values and goals." If the values of the new company were more aligned with theirs, 87% of Gen Z would switch jobs.[1] Moreover, if you hire people who share your organization's values, they'll be more likely to feel engaged in their role.

Detail their tasks and how they connect to the goals you just described

Ninety-one percent of people consider quitting a job within the first month if it doesn't match their expectations.[2] This is reason enough to be crystal clear about what you expect. Otherwise, you'll waste time and money by losing a talented hire shortly after they join.

To ensure that candidates understand how their role and responsibilities contribute to the larger mission, include a few sentences that describe how every task—even potential grunt work—has meaning behind it. For example, if one task is taking notes during team meetings, you could add an explanation like "to ensure the group stays aligned and can execute projects more efficiently."

Lay out the skills required to execute those outcomes

Don't forget to describe the specific competencies you're looking for. Which technical skills are you seeking? Which soft skills do you feel are critical to your group's success? You need to be clear about these to find candidates who can meet the requirements of the role—and deliver.

2. Nail the interview process

The next step to hiring top talent is getting the interview process right. In my experience, this requires three things: an organized and unbiased evaluation process, unique questions, and sample assignments.

Before the interviews, create a straightforward evaluation system

I recommend having a rubric that clearly defines each qualification you're looking for and a scoring system the hiring committee can use to measure the candidates in each area (see chapter 21 for a sample). You will likely be measuring candidates on a combination of soft skills like intrinsic motivation, problem-solving, adaptability, organization, and attention to detail as well as the technical skills needed to carry out the responsibilities of the role.

Assign a weight of importance to each qualification. This will help you calculate the total score for each candidate after every round of interviews. That score won't be the sole determinant of who you hire. But it will give you a process to quantify their strengths and weaknesses as seen by several teammates and help you counter the biases that show up during typical hiring decision discussions.

During the interview, ask unique questions to get authentic, unplanned responses

Here are a few favorites I've developed or learned from smart interviewers and used over the years.

- "I'll be asking candidates who advance to future rounds to provide several references, like former bosses and other people who can speak to their performance. Is that OK with you?" This revealing question can save you from a bad hire. Pay attention to body language and see who gets uncomfortable. Top talent with nothing to hide will be thrilled you're doing this diligence.

- "What are the biggest mistakes you think our company is currently making? What would you do differently?" You're testing their critical thinking, level of detailed research on your company, and confidence to speak up and challenge you.

- "Tell me about a time you disagreed with the majority of your team members. Which counterarguments altered your thinking? What would it have taken for you to have completely changed your view?" You're analyzing how open-minded they are and how willing they are to adapt or engage in high-candor debate.

- "What do you read in your spare time to sharpen your knowledge?" You're looking for signals of intellectual curiosity, a growth mindset, and the motivation to become more well-rounded.

- "If you join our team and it doesn't work out, what is the most likely reason why?" This is a creative way to tease out a potential deal breaker or weakness.

Give them a sample assignment to complete by a deadline

Choose an assignment related to the tasks they would be tackling or the problems they would be solving in the actual role, and provide them with clear, specific instructions.[3] The assignment shouldn't be too large of an ask, and it should be ethical—this is not an opportunity to get free work. Allow them to work on the assignment on their own time (not during the actual interview).

For example, when I was an institutional investor, I interviewed many analysts for my team. I would assign them a stock and ask them to conduct a full research process on the company. They had to build a financial forecast, assess the upsides and downsides of investing, and communicate their recommendation succinctly.

Sample assignments like these help you see if the candidate has the hard skills needed to succeed in the role and give you a sneak peek into the quality of their work. The result doesn't need to be perfect—you're really testing for attention to detail, punctuality, and high potential for learning and improvement.

3. Make the most of reference checks

Don't underestimate the value of reference checks—it's an opportunity to dig deeper and get the whole picture of a candidate. At the same time, because this step is often carried out by human resources, you may have to be a bit more proactive about being involved. For example, you can email your HR representative to let them know you want to gather more information on your top candidates and that speaking to their references will be essential to your final decision. If you receive any pushback, ask if you can submit a few specific questions you'd like them to ask while vetting your candidates.

Here are two strategies that can help you (or your HR team) make the most of this final step.

Put references at ease

Assure references that they have 100% confidentiality, and no comments will ever be traceable back to them. Emphasize that this reference call is one of dozens of reasons the candidate may or may not get the job. These assurances should make references more open.

Ask questions that ensure you don't get boilerplate responses

Below are the most effective reference questions I've developed or acquired from great hirers and used over time.

- "I want to balance the strengths and weaknesses of my team members. What are [name's] strengths and weaknesses, and in your experience, what kind of qualities help balance them out?" Or "What kind of teammates do they collaborate best with?"

- "How reliable and organized is [name] when it comes to getting their work done on time and accurately?"

- "When [name] disagrees with you or another person, how open-minded are they about considering another viewpoint, compromising, or adapting their view?"

- "On a scale of 1 to 10, what is your level of endorsement and why?"

When the time comes for you to make your next hire, a quick review of these essentials will position you for success.

———————

Ryan Renteria is a CEO coach, diverse board director, author of *Lead without Burnout: Growth with Less Stress for You and Your Team,* and the founder of Stretch Five, a leading executive coaching firm where he guides leaders on their journey to executing bold visions, hiring and developing top talent, achieving outstanding results, and becoming better leaders.

NOTES

1. Sophie Kiderlin, "Overwhelming Majority of Gen Z Workers Would Quit Their Jobs over Company Values, LinkedIn Data Says," CNBC, April 20 2023, https://www.cnbc.com/2023/04/20/majority -of-gen-z-would-quit-their-jobs-over-company-values-linkedin.html.

2. Robert Half, "Nine in 10 New Hires Would Leave a Job That Fails to Meet Expectations Within the First Month," roberthalf.com, June 4, 2018, https://www.roberthalf.com/gb/en/about/press/nine -10-new-hires-would-leave-job-fails-meet-expectations-within-first -month.

3. Geoff Tuff, Steve Goldbach, and Jeff Johnson, "When Hiring, Prioritize Assignments Over Interviews," hbr.org. September 27, 2022, https://hbr.org/2022/09/when-hiring-prioritize-assignments -over-interviews.

CHAPTER 2

Future-Focused Recruiting Strategies

An interview with Lauren Smith by Curt Nickisch

Remember when tech startups used to show off their catered lunches, onsite yoga instructors, and ultra-cool workspaces? Those are not such big selling points today. More people want to work remotely. It's just one of many ways that the pandemic significantly changed recruiting and hiring.

To better understand these forces, the advisory firm Gartner surveyed 3,000 job candidates and more than

Adapted from "New Recruiting Strategies for a Post-Covid World (Back to Work, Better)," March 9, 2021, *HBR IdeaCast*, podcast, season 16, episode 783.

3,500 hiring managers. The research details some of these hiring trends and points to ways that leaders can more effectively shape their workforces.

HBR: I have to admit, I was surprised at what your research found—that the pandemic didn't really disrupt recruiting and hiring as much as it accelerated trends that were already there. How is that the case?

SMITH: Three big shifts have been accelerated by the pandemic, but they definitely began before it. The first is the evolution of skills. The pace at which we work is changing, making it challenging for us to accurately define jobs. This became more universal as many organizations shifted to virtual or hybrid work, or needed to develop new types of automation.

The second big shift is the dispersion of skills beyond traditional talent pools, meaning that where we have found talent in the past isn't necessarily the best place to find it now. And the third is that candidates' expectations for their work have changed, requiring organizations to rethink how they're branding jobs and how they sell them in the labor market.

Let's start with that second one. Things have definitely changed.

They have. One of the biggest reasons is the normalization of remote work. Many organizations are no longer tied to sourcing candidates from where we've successfully found talent before and this opens up talent pools in a way that's game changing.

And of course, this also changes the calculation for candidates. Remote opportunities mean they can apply for jobs anywhere that their skills match.

What have you heard from managers looking to hire for an opening on their team? How are they experiencing this?

There was a lot of skepticism, especially for those managers who had not had virtual or remote direct reports before: "Will they be as productive?" "Can we collaborate virtually?" There's been a fair amount of surprise that individuals' ability to actually get their work done was a lot better than anticipated.

We've always thought about where people will sit when they come into a job. As if the physical space frames what that person should or shouldn't be doing. And when you're working remotely, organizations are liberated from that.

Absolutely. And it comes down to that first shift that I mentioned around the evolution of skills because so much of what managers traditionally do when hiring is look backward to the employee who has left the position. They create a job description like "I would like that past individual, plus those three other qualifications"—in essence, a purple unicorn that's very challenging for recruiters to find.

The realities of remote work and the evolution of skills means that managers can stop thinking about who they would like to hire and instead focus on the work they need done. This shift from looking at openings as an opportunity to hire to an opportunity to make a skills decision is really liberating.

Do you have a good example of an organization implementing that, and how it worked out for them?

One of the organizations we spoke with had a very interesting practice. Every time a critical role opened up, instead of going through the traditional requisition process of asking a manager to conduct the hire, the company made it a team activity. It asked the team to define the role—not what was needed in the past, but what's needed moving forward.

Not only did the team have a better understanding of the job as it was evolving on a daily basis and what was needed in terms of the interaction onsite, but they could also identify the outdated parts of the job description. So they were able to define the role in a different way.

Let's talk about the third trend your research uncovered—that candidates are increasingly selective about employers. I think that changes in recent years to the power dynamics of hiring and getting hired are really interesting. What did you see there?

Candidates increasingly expect companies to offer them not only competitive compensation and benefits, but also a compelling employee experience. People who worked remotely during lockdown got used to designing their own work experience—fitting their job into their life. Now candidates are less likely to want to give up this autonomy even if they are returning to an in-person work environment.

So we're hearing from organizations that to attract top candidates, they need to offer a more humanized deal focusing on candidates as people, not just workers. Now of course that doesn't mean you give candidates everything they want, but you do need to understand where they're coming from to make sure that you're not losing talent to competitors.

In your research, you said that companies need to address "employment value proposition."

That's right. An employment value proposition is the attributes that we offer as an organization that's going to be most attractive to candidates. And depending on the job, that's going to look very different. For some roles in knowledge work, more candidates expect flexibility. They expect a feeling of autonomy. This may mean enabling them to continue to design their work around life.

For others jobs, where such autonomy is not possible, you still need to think about how you're going to enable candidates or employees to better fit their work into their life. Scheduling flexibility is a great way.

What else are employers building into their employment value proposition?

One of the other big trends is what we've come to think of as deeper connections—understanding not just employees, but also their families and community. In lockdown, employees were working from home with small children nearby or other visible family obligations. Organizations need to continue to understand not just what their employees want, but what the people around them need.

We've seen organizations think about this in a couple of ways, whether it be opening up development opportunities to an employee's family or providing specific benefits for parents with children. So that's going to be another piece that's going to continue to evolve.

Your research pointed out that a lot of workers have taken the opportunity with their autonomy and their ability to time-shift their work to do a lot of professional development on their own, and that employers need to be aware of that.

That's right. In fact, in a survey that we ran before the pandemic, 43% of candidates said they were self-taught in one or more of the required skills for their job. So we know this has been happening for a while, but since the pandemic, there's been a boom in online learning as employees are looking to try things out beyond their current role or position themselves to be more marketable in this new environment.

It's important for organizations scanning their internal labor market to ask their employees about the skills that they have today as well as some of the skills they're hoping to build or that they're working on.

At the same time, companies need to be beefing up their ability to recruit outside of their traditional talent pools. What are some of the ways they're successfully doing that?

One of the biggest reasons that there's a lot of momentum around looking beyond traditional talent pools is that organizations are focused on advancing the diversity of their workforce. It's important to audit the current hiring process to identify where diverse candidates may be being excluded. This can be done by looking at data of recent candidates, going through the process, or creating journey maps of different candidate profiles to understand where there may be challenges.

For example, one head of recruiting I spoke with mentioned that internal talent is being excluded at pre-application because they weren't aware of existing opportunities. We've also seen examples of self-taught talent being excluded in screening because of educational requirements listed on a job description.

Really understanding where we are is important because just looking for talent in nontraditional talent pools and putting them into our existing process is not going to get the outcomes we want. For example, one hiring manager we spoke with had an interesting approach to make sure that they were looking at candidate potential over candidate credentials. It's easy to assume that great credentials or qualifications make a great candidate. But this manager looked at the skills that they needed to make sure that a candidate can grow with them over time. They landed on things like curiosity, agility, and teamwork and focused on evaluating candidates against those skills—not whether they had specific industry experience or went to one of the six schools the company traditionally recruited from.

What you're outlining makes a lot of sense. It also sounds hard, especially when companies are recruiting and hiring in a new way. HR and hiring managers haven't always been in sync. HR's often seen as a siloed part of the organization.

Absolutely. Managers who are hiring for an opening on their team and recruiting and HR leaders need to recognize that we're all on the same team looking to bring in the best talent that can move our organizations forward.

By focusing on the skills that we need to build the workforce of the future, we'll avoid just replacing the workforce we had, or getting caught in the weeds around a specific job description, or hiring a candidate because the manager went to a similar university. We need to bring the conversation back to "What do we need as an organization?" "How are we going to partner together to bring those skills in?"

I always say that HR shouldn't think of hiring as an HR activity, as a business mandate. Thinking about a manager's role around talent, not just about developing and coaching, but also their role in hiring—"How do we work together to bring in the next-generation workforce?"— makes a big difference as you think about bringing managers and HR together.

If you're a manager, what are a few things you can do the next time you look to hire somebody to really have impact?

The most important thing to do is to not just dust off the old job description when someone leaves your team. The first thing to do is document the emerging, expiring, and evolving skills associated with this role.

Emerging skills are the new things that you're going to need as the business or the nature of the team is changing. Expiring skills are those that maybe the last person had that are not as important anymore. And evolving skills is probably the most important piece. We can all think about examples of this, like learning to onboard a new team member virtually, even if you've onboarded lots of people previously.

And if a manager is able to map out the emerging, expiring, and evolving skills their team needs and bring that into a conversation with the recruiter, it's going to better position everyone to focus on *what* we're looking for, not *who* we're looking for.

––––––––––

Lauren Smith is managing vice president at Gartner. **Curt Nickisch** is a senior editor at *Harvard Business Review* where he makes podcasts and cohosts *HBR IdeaCast*.

CHAPTER 3

Forty Ideas to Shake Up Your Hiring Process

by Joseph Fuller, Nithya Vaduganathan, Allison Bailey, and Manjari Raman

Despite challenging economic conditions, companies find it difficult to attract and retain the right talent. That's one of the takeaways from a US Bureau of Labor Statistics report, which showed that job vacancies remain above 10 million as of November 2022.[1] We've confirmed that trend in our own work: when we surveyed 800 senior business leaders in August 2022, more than 95% of them told us that hiring and retaining talent

---

Adapted from "40 Ideas to Shake Up Your Hiring Process," on hbr.org, January 16, 2023 (product #H07FVQ).

was one of their top three priorities as they strive to deliver on their strategies. However, those needs are not constrained to the short term: More than two-thirds of the leaders we surveyed reported that filling positions for lower- and higher-wage workers is critical for their organization's ability to compete, both in the next 12 to 18 months and in the next three to five years.

But business leaders are doing very little that's innovative to tackle the talent challenge. When it comes to higher-wage workers, they're relying primarily on two basic strategies: increasing compensation (a fairly obvious approach) and implementing remote/hybrid work models. They're doing even less for lower-wage workers: In our survey, fewer than half of respondents reported using basic levers, such as health care benefits and compensation increases, to attract and retain these workers.

Much of this is due to a lack of awareness of innovative talent practices. Many of the leaders we surveyed simply did not know what other options were available. This, they recognized, was a problem: Fewer than 20% of them reported that their organizations had very mature talent strategies.

So how can you enable more talent innovation and measure its impact? Based on our survey findings, organizations need to use a more expansive portfolio of practices to strengthen their ability to recruit and retain talent. To help, we've identified nearly 40 strategies, which we've organized into seven categories that either strengthen the hiring process or help enhance a company's offer. Some of these practices are familiar but underutilized, and others are newer and more innovative.

Strengthening the Hiring Process

Hiring campaign and selection

Many companies rely on traditional recruiting strategies to identify candidates who fulfill a long list of requirements. Finding candidates who tick off every box on the list is not easy—and those few who do are often actually not the right people for the job. By embracing more expansive hiring and selection processes, companies can do a better job of finding the talent that's right for them. Here are some innovative practices to consider:

- Figure out what work *really* needs to get done, then rewrite job descriptions to focus on the skills and specs that matter the most for that work, instead of relying on generic education or experience requirements.

- Seek candidates who match 70% to 80% of the most critical skills for the role—and develop learning curricula to equip them with the remainder.

- Offer "micro-internships" (short-term paid projects) or apprenticeships that reach new candidate pools and allow employers and candidates to assess fit before committing to a full-time hire.

- Host open hackathons to assess talent and facilitate the hiring of candidates in batches.

- Consider candidates simultaneously for multiple open roles if they have a high number of overlapping skills.

- Leverage tech- and AI-based talent assessments to screen for technical or interpersonal skills.

- Employ inclusive, gender-neutral language in job descriptions to attract more diverse candidates.

Talent sourcing

When competition for top talent is fierce, as it is today, you need to broaden your methods of sourcing candidates. Here are some practices to consider:

- Expand internal talent mobility (e.g., lateral job transfers, internal gig work) by drawing on a foundation of skills and aspirations as a basis for mobility and supporting retention.

- Embrace on-demand and gig platforms to increase labor force flexibility (even for higher-wage workers), accelerate time-to-market, and enable innovation.

- Work to attract alumni with valuable institutional knowledge back to your organization.

- Build an internal list of previously high-performing employees who might be candidates to reengage for future roles.

- Tap into "hidden" populations, including retired, neurodiverse, and previously incarcerated workers.

- Acquire companies with top talent—or enter into agreements to borrow and share talent with other companies.

Channel strategy

Companies that integrate new and innovative channels into their talent strategy can better recruit critical, in-demand talent for years to come. Consider expanding your repertoire to include the following techniques:

- Deploy talent from Hire-Train-Deploy (HTD) partners who source high-potential candidates and equip them with the relevant skills for your needs.

- Use digital platforms to do more programmatic and personalized recruiting (including leveraging QR codes, text messaging).

- Partner with educational and community institutions, including job centers and community colleges, to offer tailored curriculum and term-time work experiences to build a talent pipeline with relevant skills.

- Embrace new ways of identifying talent on social media platforms (such as layoff lists and LinkedIn posts).

- Develop and market a more effective referral program, particularly for in-demand roles.

Enhancing the Offer

Compensation and benefits

Are you one of the many employers raising salaries to compete for talent? Half of the 800+ respondents in our survey reported increasing compensation for their employees, and nearly 75% of employers cite the talent shortage as the main driver for salary budget increases.[2] But there are other ways to strengthen your compensation and benefits package. Try some of these practices to get started:

- Provide creative benefits, such as caregiver support programs, childcare services, and wellness perks.

- Segment and develop tailored benefits for hard-to-fill talent populations.

- Provide incentives, such as higher bonuses during peak hours and step-ups on promotion, especially for lower-wage workers.

- Guarantee health care benefits and appropriate sick time for your full workforce.

- Reduce volatility by ensuring stable and predictable pay, particularly for lower-wage workers.

Work Design

Job flexibility has skyrocketed in importance since the onset of the pandemic, with some employees valuing flexibility even more than a 10% pay raise. Rethinking work design can not only better attract and retain workers but can also increase productivity and focus worker capacity on the highest-value tasks. Get started redesigning work with the following strategies:

- Break work into its components to assign responsibilities more clearly across a team or to freelance workers, and improve your approach to sourcing.

- Deploy talent more dynamically by creating skills-based talent pools that can be assigned to the most critical priorities on demand.

- Use creative scheduling and shift redesign to allow lower-wage workers to move or switch shifts more flexibly while still providing adequate coverage.

- Experiment with different flex models, including compressed workweeks, sharing jobs among multiple part-time employees, and/or scheduling split shifts to cover "rush hours."

- Redesign work by eliminating, reassigning, or automating less-critical responsibilities.

- Embed technology that improves ease of work, including language assistance and tools to accommodate older workers.

Career development

Providing opportunities for your employees to take on stretch assignments can help you not only develop but also retain your employees. According to the Pew Research Center, more than 60% of US employees cited a lack of career-advancement opportunities as a leading reason for leaving their jobs.[3] To expand your organization's portfolio of career-advancement opportunities, consider adding some of these innovative practices:

- Provide education benefits linked to individualized skill development plans (for example, tuition reimbursement).

- Build targeted learning and development programs to support onboarding, upskilling, and reskilling across both hard and soft skills.

- Design mentorship and sponsorship programs and peer-to-peer coaching systems.

- Upskill managers to be better people leaders and increase manager accountability for team development.

Culture

Companies need a compelling culture to maximize the engagement, productivity, and retention of their existing workforces. In recent years, company culture has become the most important driver of job satisfaction, with culture being 10 times more predictive of employee retention than compensation.[4] Here are some innovative practices to help build a meaningful culture:

- Embed company purpose, strategy, and values in your operating and performance practices and feedback process, and train your leaders to become culture champions.

- Set up robust onboarding programs that build affiliation and mentorship into the process.

- Create opportunities and free up as much as 10% to 20% of capacity for passion projects.

- Boost affiliation by developing interest groups and communities of practice.

- Take pulse checks on employee sentiment to highlight opportunities for improvement in near real time.

- Develop clear two-way communication channels for employee input and engagement.

The best talent strategy for your organization involves finding the right portfolio of practices that meet your needs and investing appropriately in their implementation, even during uncertain economic conditions. Many companies across industries have recognized how critical talent is to business success and have kickstarted their innovation journeys based on their target employee needs. For example, IBM removed degree requirements from 50% of their U.S. job postings to widen their talent pools, Walmart provides frontline associates with fully funded college tuition and accelerated career paths after graduation, and some law firms have introduced concierge services to support aging family members.[5]

While you don't have to do everything on our list to have a successful talent strategy, you should identify where you can do more to better compete for talent. Take stock of what your organization is already doing, then thoughtfully assess where there are gaps in your talent strategy and how our suggestions can be helpful. Keep in mind that you may need to tailor your talent strategies to different employee segments within your company. By experimenting with new innovations and putting the right feedback systems in place, you can develop a sustainable strategy that can help you create lasting talent advantage.

Acknowledgements: *We would like to thank Colleen McDonald, partner, and Christina Li, consultant, both with Boston Consulting Group, for their contributions to this piece.*

————————

Joseph Fuller is a professor of management practice and a faculty cochair of the Project on Managing the Future of Work at Harvard Business School.

Nithya Vaduganathan is a managing director and partner at the Boston Consulting Group, a leader in BCG's People and Organization and Education practices, and a Henderson Institute Fellow on new talent models.

Allison Bailey is a senior partner and a managing director at BCG. She leads the firm's People & Organization practice globally and is a coauthor of several publications on the future of work, the bionic company, digital learning, and upskilling. She is also a fellow of the BCG Henderson Institute.

Manjari Raman is a senior program director and a senior researcher for Harvard Business School's U.S. Competitiveness Project and the Project on Managing the Future of Work.

NOTES

1. "Job Openings and Labor Turnover—May 2024," Bureau of Labor Statistics, US Department of Labor, https://www.bls.gov/news .release/pdf/jolts.pdf.

2. Trey Williams, "U.S. Companies Are Raising Salary Budgets the Most Since the Great Recession," *Fortune*, July 15, 2022, https:// fortune.com/2022/07/15/u-s-companies-raise-salary-budgets-amid -inflation-concerns/.

3. Kim Parker and Juliana Menasce Horowitz, "Majority of Workers Who Quit a Job in 2021 Cite Low Pay, No Opportunities for Advancement, Feeling Disrespected," Pew Research Center, March 9, 2022, https://www.pewresearch.org/short-reads/2022/03/09/majority -of-workers-who-quit-a-job-in-2021-cite-low-pay-no-opportunities-for -advancement-feeling-disrespected/.

4. Tom Miller, "Shaping a Culture That Will Retain Employees," *Executive Network*, SHRM, March 8, 2022, https://www.shrm.org/ executive-network/insights/shaping-culture-will-retain-employees#:~: text=Right%20now%2C%20company%20culture%20is,decides%20 to%20leave%20their%20job.

5. "How the US Can Lead in Education and Build a More Equitable Economy," IBM, January 28, 2021, https://www.ibm.com/policy/ education-skills/; Amy Goldfinger, "At Walmart, There Is a Path for Everyone," Walmart, May 15, 2022, https://corporate.walmart .com/news/2022/05/15/at-walmart-there-is-a-path-for-everyone; Kathryn Mayer, "Employers Turn to Eldercare to Help Workers During COVID," *Human Resource Executive*, September 11, 2020, https://hrexecutive.com/companies-turn-to-eldercare-benefits-to -help-workers-during-covid-19/.

CHAPTER 4

Imagine a Better Hiring Process

by Alex Haimann

Shortly after we started hiring for our business, we recognized how deeply flawed traditional interview processes are. At the time, we had a goal of growing our CRM software company from six to 18 employees. Our objectives were simple: Find talented people to contribute to our culture, generate great work, and stay with us for the long term. We decided to focus on optimizing our interview process rather than relying on outdated behavioral questions.

Think of the classic prompts: *What are your greatest strengths and weaknesses? Tell me about a time you overcame a challenge at work.*

Adapted from "How to Design a Better Hiring Process" on hbr.org, June 26, 2020 (product #H05OZ9).

The standard interview is a tradition of sorts that has been passed down from one generation to another. But, as we discovered through our own missteps, it is unreliable.[1] Behavioral questions might be useful for testing someone's ability to relay biographical information. However, unless storytelling or some equivalent skill is a requirement of the position being filled, they often fail to reveal sufficient information about a candidate's competencies.

You don't need outside consultants or a robust HR function to hire like a pro. Through trial and error, my team and I have used our own experiences, as well as the most recent research available, to create a process that immerses job candidates in unconventional scenarios to gather the most useful insights about their critical-thinking abilities, tech savviness, and interpersonal skills.

Since deployment, we have seen improvements both in the quality of our hires and what they bring to the company. As a result, our retention has improved significantly. In the past seven years, we've had only four full-time employees leave—two for grad school and two for jobs outside of our industry.

Today, we believe that what worked for us can work for other companies too, saving your organization both time and money by finding the right people for the right roles.

This is the process that works for us; let some of the ideas inspire you to adopt or adapt for your own organization and culture.

Part 1: Questions

First, it's important to note that our process varies. We aim to structure our interviews around the skills we're looking for from each candidate and give them the opportunity to demonstrate those skills. Because no two candidates are the same, naturally, neither are two interviews.

Prior to *all* of our interviews, we share the questions we'll be asking with candidates. We ask these questions during the conversational portion of the interview, which comes first and takes 45 to 90 minutes. We're intentionally flexible with time here to allow for whatever subsequent discussions may arise.

Typically, our questions are broken down into three categories:

1. To test for **preparation**, we ask questions that are easy to research. For example, "Can you tell us what you know about our company?" is something that a quick Google search could answer.

2. To test for **critical thinking and tech savviness**, we ask open-ended questions designed to start a conversation and spark creativity in the candidate. For example, we often ask engineering candidates how they would design an app to accomplish a certain task (view pictures of animals, for instance). We ask customer service or salesperson candidates to choose a piece of software they are familiar with and demo it. For a video interview, we'd give the candidate rights to share and ask them to take over and demonstrate the product. During an in-office interview, we would ask the candidate to control the mouse and keyboard to demo the software on a large monitor while we watch.

3. To test for **listening and communication skills**, we format some questions as directions. This gives candidates a clear idea of what we want from them, while at the same time allowing us to see whether they can deliver. For example, to measure a candidate's ability to communicate effectively, we might say: "Teach us about one of your passions, something that you know a lot about or consider yourself to be a nominal expert in—and teach us as if we know nothing about it."

Many of our questions in categories 2 and 3 allow candidates to pick the topics of discussion themselves, as opposed to us thrusting ideas on them. We aspire to stimulate a discussion that they (hopefully) want to engage in. If candidates choose topics they don't know much about or aren't able to explain, despite having time to prepare beforehand, it shows us that they didn't care enough about the interview or the position to put in the time. Essentially, we want our hires to have the ability to think ahead and draw on real knowledge and experience in high-pressure situations. What we don't want is to hire people simply because they have a knack for saying what they think we want to hear.

Video interviews help us measure online communication skills. We can determine a candidate's tech savviness with programs like Zoom, as well as how they present themselves over video—an important skill, as this is how many members of our team interact with prospects, customers, and other employees.

Part 2: Technical Skills

After the question portion of the interview, we schedule a 45- to 90-minute chat between the candidate and a team member who is an expert in their field, followed by a short exercise to test their collaboration skills.

During the chat, our team members typically ask candidates role-specific questions to help us gauge whether they have a genuine interest in the work they'd be doing. With customer service positions, for example, we ask candidates whether they think helping people is rewarding, whether they like talking on the phone, and so on. Depending on the candidate and the flow of that interview, we might also ask less direct, general questions about their interests and what work they find most rewarding. If our hires love the work they are doing, we've found, they are more likely to stay for the long term.

For the exercise portion of this stage, we aim to create scenarios that will allow us to see candidates' skills in action and evaluate how well they collaborate with other employees. This time also gives the candidate an opportunity to experience what it would be like to work on a specific team. For instance, we may ask an engineering candidate to participate in pair programming—a technique in which two developers work together on a problem. While pair programming is a common practice in many coding job interviews, we've incorporated similar team exercises into the interviews for all of our roles.

As with part one of the interview, we let candidates know beforehand which topics will be covered in the technical portion, as it puts the onus on them to come prepared. Videoconferencing technology that incorporates elements like screen-sharing and tools designed specifically for remote code interviews, such as Code-Bunk, can be helpful in conducting these exercises virtually.

Part 3: Writing Samples

Many companies collect writing samples from candidates before or after an initial interview. But we believe it is more beneficial to govern this process more closely because it gives us insight into the quality of a candidate's writing without any outside assistance. We want to know that all our hires will be able to communicate clearly in writing without extensive editing and sometimes under time pressure. Though we can't ensure that people aren't seeking outside assistance (such as AI), our process still gives us a good idea of their writing and communication skills.

The assignment we give is specific to the role each candidate is applying for. For example, we give customer service candidates a sample email from a hypothetical angry client, as well as an example email response that reflects our ideal company voice. We ask that they mimic the company voice and write up a client response email of their own. We also expect them to ask as many questions as possible beforehand—and take notes. We don't specify the length of response, but the example gives them a good idea of our expectations.

In the office, we typically give candidates 30 to 45 minutes in a quiet room to complete the writing assignment. Virtually, we would schedule a break in our video call to give them 30 to 45 minutes to complete the assignment. After they've finished, we would resume the interview online as we review the assignment and ask why they chose certain phrasing or structures in their response. When we review the sample, we look at whether they can think critically about composition and voice and demonstrate thoughtfulness overall.

Part 4: Games

We want to know how candidates will interact with their prospective colleagues on a day-to-day basis. But instead of making assumptions based on their answers to interview questions—like "How would your coworkers describe you?" or "What role do you tend to play on a team?"—our process allows us to observe their actual interactions.

In the office, we design peer interactions around board games that challenge players to work together toward a goal, as opposed to games that pit players against one another in a zero-sum scenario. Virtually, we would go with a game, such as Codenames, that's easier to play in a remote setting, but still allows for that key element of collaboration. The goal is twofold: Learn about how the candidate interacts with team members *and* show them that this will be a fun place to work.

Because candidates interact with numerous employees throughout our interview process, many of whom don't share their backgrounds or interests, we find team members who might have more in common with them for this portion of the interview. While it's important for us to make sure the candidate can engage with a diverse group of our employees, during this time specifically, we want them to feel comfortable, conversational, and included.

If our current team is made up of individuals over the age of 45, for instance, and we're interviewing a recent college graduate, we don't necessarily look for the youngest person in the office to include in this step. Instead, we might look to include the newest, least experienced members of our team, regardless of age, to help the candidate feel more comfortable and less intimidated by experienced employees.

The outcome of the game isn't important. We're looking for signs of a good cultural fit over the course of the three to four hours the players are together. For us, that means candidates are thoughtful, engaging, curious, and make a visible effort to enjoy the experience (even if they are faking it). These attributes aren't role-specific; they're qualities we value as a company.

Quantify What's Working and What's Not

The four pillars above require regular iteration and experimentation. After each round of hiring, we sit down to evaluate the success of our process by looking at a couple of different factors. One of these is how often each pillar swayed our decision. Were we able to make more confident choices using these steps? If so, we take that as validation that the process is working. If not, we take a deeper look at what's not working and how we can fix it.

The most important factor we use to evaluate the success of our process, though, is the quality of our hires. A couple of years ago, when we realized we had hired many interns who were perfectly capable of doing their work but weren't actually interested in the work itself, we knew we had a quality problem to address. Some interns told us during exit interviews that they were just using the internship as a stepping-stone for their next destination, and some declined full-time job offers from us.

That's when we began drafting up more role-specific questions to ask candidates during the technical portion of the interview. Only then did we see our retention grow stronger.

Our post-interview evaluation is another element of the process we had to adjust. Initially, staff members talked to each other about the candidate throughout the interview day (without the candidate present) and compared experiences. But we found this created bias and other conflicts throughout the interview itself.

Now we forbid employees to talk with anyone about the candidate until after the interview is completed. Once it is, everyone who participated completes a survey with feedback about the various areas we assessed. After everyone has filled out the survey, we allow open discussion.

It may be tempting for some leaders to simply accept that hiring is not a perfect science and use that as an excuse to stick with the same outdated interview process corporations have relied on for decades. But today it's safe to say that most businesses can't afford to take a chance on bad hires. We think it's possible to design an interview process that provides a clear assessment of a candidate's skills, aptitude, and potential for culture fit. Our four pillars can be used as a framework for those who wish to do so.

———————

Alex Haimann is a partner and the head of business development at Less Annoying CRM, a simple CRM built from the ground up for small businesses. Over 10,000 small businesses worldwide use LACRM to manage contacts, track leads, and stay on top of follow-ups. LACRM continues to grow by engaging customers and finding new opportunities for mutually beneficial partnerships.

NOTE

1. Laszlo Bock, "Here's Google's Secret to Hiring the Best People," *Wired*, April 7, 2015, https://www.wired.com/2015/04/hire-like-google/.

CHAPTER 5

Six Critical Ways HR Assists with Recruiting and Hiring

by Roxanne Calder

"Hiring talent" rarely appears at the top of a manager's job description or is even included as a required competency. Maybe that's because it's an "assumed skill" that one acquires via experience and exposure at a certain career stage or as a task to delegate to HR ("Put in a call to HR and leave it with them!") or outsource to a recruiter. But that's not how it works. As a recruiter with over two decades of experience, I know that successful recruitment requires effective collaboration between HR and hiring managers.

It's not always easy working with functional teams—people you collaborate with only on occasion. When it comes to HR, it can feel almost personal. How can you trust that they understand the role you're trying to fill? What if they send the wrong people (or no one at all!)? To hire great people for your team, you must establish and maintain a strong relationship with HR. You'll need to draw on your collaboration skills and work together to understand each other's priorities, responsibilities, skill sets, and communication styles and preferences. Keeping an open mind, listening actively, and communicating frequently and consistently will be key to a successful partnership.

Though the ways of working will vary from company to company, most HR teams act as a guide through the recruiting and hiring process, advising on best practices at each stage. HR can be very hands-on, sitting in on all interviews and participating in candidate evaluations, or very hands-off, providing policies and advice and leaving you to it.

While every organization has its own process and culture, here's the high-level view of how to build an effective partnership with HR to identify, evaluate, and add great people to your team.

Lay the Groundwork

The recruitment process isn't static. It can involve many people, a lot of moving parts, changing minds and differing opinions, and new information entering the fray. The better you partner with HR to prepare *before* posting the job, the more agile and confident you can be in responding to questions throughout the process and the better you'll be able to deliver a compelling offer and speedy contract when you've made your final selection.

Obtain approval

The first step you'll take with HR is to secure approval of the job requisition. Many companies require authorization before recruitment can start (this is usually due to budgeting and headcount restrictions, especially during more challenging economic times). Your HR department can advise you on your company's approval process: whether it requires board, managing director, or CEO-level sign-off, even if the role is a replacement. Sign-off may take one day or two weeks—even months—and there's a chance that it can be refused altogether. Make sure you've got the needed approval before you start meeting with candidates. Generating a contract and final offer letter takes time, and if you have to backtrack for approval at the end of the process, you run the real risk of losing talent—not to mention damage to your company's reputation and your personal brand.

Understand the full package

Once you have approval to hire, you'll work with HR to understand the total remuneration package. This includes the salary range, benefits, and growth opportunities. Knowing the numbers—including the maximum level you're able to offer—will save you time and avoid having to reopen the approval process. Your HR partner can help you get a strong handle on the benefits your company offers, as well as any perks, and how they translate to dollars. If you're a nonprofit and have salary tax concessions, work to understand what this means in terms of earnings.

You'll also want to review with HR all critical policies, such as working from home, remote work, well-being, parental leave, and so on. If at any stage in the process, your candidate asks a question about any of these matters—including salary—a confident, well-articulated response portrays professionalism and confidence, and goes a long way to establishing trust.

Conduct market research

Beyond your own organization, you'll want to step back to look at the context of the wider market. Failure to understand the employment landscape can lead to losing out on great candidates or making hiring mistakes. If HR hasn't provided you with market and industry information about similar roles, they can help you find it. Once you know the remuneration package you can offer, look at job boards and salary guides or reach out to expert recruiters to check that it is aligned with the market. Taking the existing salary of the incumbent and assuming it's at the right level is easy but won't always be accurate if you haven't recruited for the role in a while (even within the last 12 months).

If, after comparing the salary package with the market, you find that what you're offering isn't competitive, you may need a backup plan. Consider what else you can incorporate into the offer to make it more attractive. Look to cultural elements and unique selling points such as summer hours or professional development opportunities. Additionally, revisit the job description. Are there criteria, skills, or experience levels you can compromise on to match the salary level instead?

Review the job description

A good job description is the official document used as a reference point for everyone involved and captures all the essential skills and tasks required. It's not a wish list or a job manual. Work with HR when you craft the job description. Your HR partner may provide templates or samples. Use them to capture all key elements of the job to ensure that you and HR and anyone on the hiring team are in alignment. Detail your expectations for the role, including the cultural fit—what does and doesn't work in your team, and why. Evaluate and discuss with HR all requirements, tasks, and responsibilities. For each skill, background, and experience requirement, ask "Why?" Unnecessary requirements confuse priorities, making it harder to find the right person. HR can assist in identifying the essential skills.

Clarify your deal-breakers for candidates with HR as well. If you insist on timely follow-up with clients, high attention to detail, weekly updates on progress, say so. Your HR partner might suggest additional tests or interview questions to help you home in on candidates with the skills and attributes that are most important to you. Keep an open mind and listen to the advice HR shares with you. At this juncture, you'll also discuss possible internal candidates and employee referrals and related policies. Some companies require advertising jobs internally before going to market. Your HR partner will be able to help you identify and reach out to possible internal candidates and ensure that you follow your company's procedures for posting jobs.

These conversations are an opportunity to be frank and to build trust with your HR business partner. If HR is involved in interviewing and selecting candidates, its people need to acutely understand the right fit for you. Spend the time now so you're both on the same page. Document everything in the job description. If this is a replacement role, ensure that the description aligns with any changes to the job requirements.

Make a plan

You and your HR partner have worked long and hard to think through what you need and how best to position the role. It's time to map out everything in a recruiting and hiring plan. This record doesn't have to be formal or long; your company may use a specific template or form. This is your opportunity to capture your decisions and approach to ensure alignment of goals and expectations. In the plan, specify how many rounds of interviews each candidate will go through, and which people will interview candidates and at what stage. Note all key tasks and timelines and add tips for best practice. For example, if interviews are to occur within a certain time frame (e.g., five days from receipt of résumé) or time from screening to interview (e.g., two days). Block out ample time in your own calendar for screening and interviewing. Consider when you need someone to start. Is there enough time for overlap to arrange a handover? If not, speak with HR about backup and transition plans. Perhaps look to a contractor in the interim or other employees who might view helping out as a growth and learning opportunity.

If concerns crop up during the process, the recruiting and hiring plan acts as your review document. For example, if after one month, you haven't sourced your candidate, instead of a panicked or frustrated conversation, use the plan as your checkpoint and as a tool to navigate a difficult conversation. Where along the process was best practice not followed? "Oh, we took three weeks to process the ad response when we had only committed to one." Reviewing and discussing the plan with your HR partner can help you identify and discuss any issues and work to address them.

Recruit and Screen

Once you've secured all approvals; documented the key skills, abilities, and tasks related to the role and done your homework to understand the package you're offering, you'll work with your HR partner to get your ad in front of job seekers and begin building a pool of candidates.

Write the job ad

A job advertisement is different from a job description. A job description outlines the requirements, whereas the ad *sells* your job. A job ad should outline the main responsibilities and tasks as well as key attractions of the role and organization—the values and culture. Don't dump lists of tasks or monotonous duties into it. Do include items such as training, learning, and career opportunities. HR can assist with writing appropriate copy, including any boilerplate text and avoiding discriminatory language. Ensure that whatever is in the ad is authentic. For example, if you mention that the role is hybrid, be prepared to discuss and explain what that means on your team. If your company process allows you to include the salary band in the ad, prepare to articulate what warrants the higher level as opposed to the lower end. A thoughtful answer to this question will help you establish trust with candidates.

When the language is worked out to everyone's satisfaction, HR can also suggest platforms to use for posting the ad.

Review résumés

Effectively managing the influx of applications requires sharp coordination. Screening should be conducted as soon as résumés are received. Your ideal candidate might be number 84 on the list of résumés, but not accessing them for five days could see them take another role. HR might suggest using AI to help to make screening more efficient and to reduce bias. Work out a process and timeline with HR for receiving screened résumés so you'll have time to review them. If you're responsible for screening all résumés, allow ample time to sift through them. Use the job description as the basis of your screening questions, ensuring that all candidates tick the main criteria before advancing to the interview round.

Book interviews

Once you screen suitable candidates, schedule their interviews straight away, even as soon as the following day.

The allotted time varies according to industry and job level; ideally, however, an interview should be booked as timely and efficiently as possible.

Conduct Interviews

With a pared-down list of candidates, it's time to activate the interview plan you established with HR. Your HR partner can help you coordinate and schedule the people involved in the interview process, ensuring that you follow your established plan, stick to company policies and procedures, and work around everyone's availability within the desired time frame. Of course, the interview is where you'll learn about the candidate's ability to do the job, but it's also a great time to build trust and begin to gather candidate-specific information that will help you make an appropriate offer later on.

Establish or affirm the process

As you engage and activate your hiring panel, your goal is to create value and not erode efficiency. Work with HR to establish a mechanism to receive timely feedback, evaluations, and scorecards from the hiring team. Allow time for discussion of candidate suitability. If multiple people are involved in the decision-making, you'll want to build in extra time for discussions, the increased work required to consolidate the feedback, and the challenge of coordinating competing calendars.

Refine and select questions

Because of the time you invested early on, working with HR to design and select interview questions to draw out candidates' skills, competencies, and cultural fit should be a fairly swift and focused process. Use the updated job description as the basis for questions. HR can advise on how to frame questions, what to look for in the answers, tips to help you probe further, and red flags to watch for.

Talk about money

In the interview, state the salary range of your job up front and ask what the candidate is expecting. Now is the time to test the waters and understand if your expectations are aligned and if not, why. Ask about their current salary and benefits and the last time they received a pay increase. Their salary may already be at the higher level of what you can offer, but if you discover they only recently received the increase, it can help you to position your offering, perhaps with other benefits or a commitment to review the salary at the next performance appraisal.

Ask why they're on the job market

Use the interview to find out why the candidate is leaving their current role. If they're on the market due to a lack of learning and development opportunities at their current company and this is something you can provide, knowing this detail will strengthen your offer. Learning more about what they're looking for is also important for hiring for the long term. Cultural fit matters in attracting the right people, having offers accepted, and ensuring engagement and retention.

Find out who you're up against

In addition to understanding why your candidate is leaving their current position, you'll also want to know where else they're looking. Where else are they interviewing? What roles and salaries are they pursuing? Don't be afraid to ask how the other roles compare to yours—this will help you gauge if you're in the running or not. Find out what stage they're at in the hiring process elsewhere. Say they're at final interview stage at another organization; if you think they're the right candidate, you may want to work with HR and your hiring team to speed up your process to secure them.

Keep in touch

One of the biggest complaints from candidates is the lack of communication and follow-up from hiring managers during the interview process. So work with HR to identify who will communicate with all candidates and how, even if it's only a brief update. Relaying the status and stage of the process is respectful and helps build good relationships. If someone is no longer being considered, let them know as soon as possible.

Make a Choice

After screening and interviewing candidates, you're making your way toward selecting who you'll hire. Often hiring managers relax at this stage, thinking they've found their ideal person. But guess what? Until your candidate has signed a contract, they haven't found their ideal job. And if the recruitment stage requires speed, selection becomes supersonic. HR can help keep you on track and coordinate feedback in this exciting and fast-moving phase of the process.

Wrapup interviews and assessments

Once you've narrowed down the selection, book the second-round interviews with your team as well as any follow-up interviews or testing that might be required. Delays open the door for candidates to interview else-where and take other positions.

Gather all feedback

Collate feedback and scorecards from your hiring panel. Discuss your most promising candidates with HR and other stakeholders. This may require additional discussions. If you are fortunate to have a good pool of candidates, it's also prudent to determine who the backup candidate might be.

Consider pre-closing

When you get to a final interview with your selected candidate, you may want to conduct a "pre-close" where you verbally offer the job, barring any last-minute red flags that arise in this final meeting. If things have continued to go well, pose a hypothetical question: If they were offered the role, would they accept? If they say no or they're not sure, ask them what might stop them from accepting the role. If they say yes, you can then present the verbal offer you have prepared with HR.

Make an Offer

At last, you've found your winning candidate! You breathe a sigh of relief. All that needs to be done is to present the offer. But what if they start negotiating, asking for more money or extra benefits or time off before starting? If you feel yourself putting off your answer and becoming a little queasy, you're not alone. I refer to this stage of the recruitment process as the pointy end. You don't want to stall, relax, or falter. You need to switch it up a gear. The rapport, relationship, and trust you've worked to establish during the process are key in getting offers across the line. With the right preparation and assistance from HR, presenting and negotiating the offer can be a breeze.

Understand what's involved in an offer

An offer is the compensation package, including salary and benefits, that you present to your candidate. There are generally two stages. First there is the verbal offer, where you state your intention to hire the person and name the salary details, either face-to-face or over a phone or video call. This generally happens in the final interview or within the following one to three days. The formal offer, generally a letter and contract detailing the salary and benefits and timeline, follows the verbal offer and is usually delivered by email, post, or courier. The optimal timeline for the formal offer is one to two days after you've presented the verbal offer, although the same day is ideal.

Keep HR in the loop

Even though you've been in touch with HR throughout the whole hiring process, the formal offer of the contract can still take time to generate. If this comes from your HR team, advise them as soon as you have decided on your candidate and let them know that you intend to make a verbal offer.

Present the offer

It's best practice for the offer to be made by you, the manager, since you've been involved from the start. By the time you get to the decision and offer stage, you have built the foundation for a relationship with your future employee. Plus, you've been in conversations, listening deeply to capture the precious nuggets of information that might help tailor and influence the offer. For example, if your candidate mentioned an area of training that was of interest to them, you could investigate the course ahead of time and be able to describe how your company could support it financially or otherwise.

The first offer should be verbal and strong. A talent-tight market is not one in which to lowball, whether it's happening as a pre-close in a final interview or as a follow-up after all interview rounds have been completed. Your HR team can help you prepare for this conversation, but you might open by saying, "I am delighted to offer you the role with us; the salary is XXX." Be warm and enthusiastic. Share why you're looking forward to working with them. Inquire if they have any questions.

Ask for a verbal acceptance

Once you've delivered the verbal offer, ask if they're happy to accept based on the details you've provided. This is yet another pre-close: "Are you happy to accept?" You're looking for an affirmation. Responses such as, "I'd like to take a few days to think it over" should sound alarm bells for you and prompt you to try to learn more.

Probe for more details

If your candidate asks for time to think your offer over, ask what areas require consideration. If they remain steadfast, use your judgment. Sometimes people really do need more time. If that's the case, applying pressure won't assist and might turn them away. However, if you're concerned the offer won't be accepted, you may want to revert to your backup plan, keeping HR in the loop. If the candidate mentioned in the interview process that they were exploring other job opportunities, ask again where they are in process with those companies and who they're waiting to hear back from. Ask if they will be turning down other offers. You want to hear yes, of course. These might seem uncomfortable questions to ask, but they're necessary. Don't stick your head in the sand, hoping all will be OK. It's better to know because it will give you time to counter other offers and negotiate a successful offer.

Negotiate terms—or not

Sometimes candidates will want to negotiate. Put yourself in their shoes and consider their viewpoint and motivations. You have done the work to prepare, so you know how far you can go with the salary, what the market is like, and the value of your potential new hire.

Sometimes, it's better to stick with what you believe is the right and fair original offer, especially if it was a strong one. If you're pushing back, do so in a way that makes your potential new hire feel OK for asking. It takes courage to talk about money and negotiate. You want any employee to feel comfortable to come to you for any matter in the future. Acknowledge the request, thank them for being open with you, and either share the reason you can't deliver what they have asked for or, if you believe what they are asking for is fair, agree. When discussing these points, be sure to mention the additional benefits that may be offered—such as free lunches, flexible hours, seasonal bonuses, training, and so on— that may be as attractive as a higher salary.

Update HR

After you've reached a verbal agreement, share the details with HR so they can generate the official letter and contract.

Check references

With your verbal agreement on the terms of the job, get your candidate's permission to conduct reference checks. It's no longer best practice to check the references of multiple candidates. It's time-consuming and inefficient. The process can be outsourced to an external body or performed by HR or yourself, but I recommend that managers conduct these themselves, as it can provide additional insights into new hires. All reference checks should be completed as soon as possible and before the formal contract and letter of offer are issued. If references cannot be completed straight away, this may delay finalizing and delivering the contract, so keep your candidate up to date.

Close the Deal

The recruitment process isn't over until your person starts!

Deliver the official offer and contract

Once references are completed, send the contract and letter of offer. These constitute the official offer, outlining the necessary information and legalities. Typically, these documents are generated by HR and can be sent via HR or you as hiring manager. I suggest they come from you, with a phone call advising that the package is on its way. Ideally, the contract should go out the same day as the verbal offer, but sometimes there are delays in securing references so update your candidate as necessary.

Address last-minute negotiations

Even when the offer is set in ink, candidates will sometimes try to negotiate more money or make other changes. You have the salary banding and market information you gathered earlier in the process, so you know what is reasonable to negotiate. For contract changes, HR will know what is and isn't possible. Generally, HR will oversee the signing and take over the documentation from there.

Stay in touch

Keep in regular contact with your new hire even after the contract has been signed and returned during their notice period, including if they're taking additional time before starting. They may continue to receive recruitment calls even if they've stopped actively applying. Additionally, if they're good at what they do, expect their existing employer to try and convince them to stay, right up until the last minute. This is why building a relationship with your candidate and keeping in touch are keys to successfully signing your chosen candidate and seeing them start in their new role.

What If Your Search Doesn't Yield a Final Candidate?

Sometimes a search can wind down without finding the right person. If this happens, look to the backup plan you created with HR for an interim solution. Review the documented process plan for learning opportunities. Recruitment is not easy; even undertaken with the best of skills and intentions, it can go awry. Determine if you start again with a different plan, or consider engaging an expert recruiter. Working with a recruitment agency is not a concession of failure but a strategic enhancement of the hiring process. It reflects a commitment to securing the best talent through all available means. Leveraging the unique skills, networks, and insights of recruitment agencies can transform a challenging hiring process into a success story.

Gone are the days of making a job offer and simply having it accepted. Working with HR to scope, recruit, and hire for your team is a delicate and complex dance. Thorough preparation, effective communication, and collaborative partnership will help you identify and hire the candidate whose skills and abilities will move your team and your organization forward.

———————

Roxanne Calder, author of *Employable: 7 Attributes to Assure Your Working Future* (Major Street, 2022), is the founder and managing director of EST10—one of Sydney's most successful recruitment agencies. For more information on how Roxanne can assist with your recruitment needs, visit www.est10.com.au.

CHAPTER 6

Reduce Personal Bias in the Hiring Process

by Ruchika T. Malhotra

When it comes to hiring candidates from underestimated backgrounds, good intentions do not necessarily lead to good results. I once met a talent acquisition leader at a large global technology company who had changed the organization's hiring process in multiple ways to bring in more candidates of color but was frustrated by the lack of progress. Internal analyses showed that even though the company had interviewed a higher

---

Adapted from "How to Reduce Personal Bias When Hiring" on hbr.org, June 28, 2019 (product #H05105).

number of non-white candidates in preliminary rounds, their final hires were still overwhelmingly white.

I've seen this same situation play out in multiple organizations and industries, and often it's because well-intentioned hiring managers end up inadvertently weeding out qualified candidates from underestimated backgrounds because of bias.

Changes in process and diversity initiatives alone are not going to remedy the lack of equal representation in companies. Individual managers who are often making the final hiring decisions need to address their own bias.

But how? In my experience, there are several things you, as a hiring manager, can do.

Before taking any steps, however, it's important to accept that no one is preloaded with inclusive behavior; we are, in fact, biologically hardwired to align with people like us and reject those whom we consider different.

Undoing these behaviors requires moving from a fixed mindset—the belief that we're already doing the best we possibly can to build diverse teams—to one of openness and growth, where we can deeply understand, challenge, and confront our personal biases.

Here are the specific strategies I recommend.

Accept that you have biases, especially affinity bias

Even if you head up your organization's diversity committee, even if you are from an underrepresented community, you have biases that impact your professional decisions, especially hiring. *Affinity bias*—having a more favorable opinion of someone like us—is one of the most common.[1] In hiring, this often means referring or selecting a candidate who shares our race or gender, or who went to the same school, speaks the same language, or reminds us of our younger selves.

Microsoft's corporate vice president of HR, Chuck Edward, told me that affinity bias is widespread in hiring and often leads people to seek out and hire candidates who "look, act, and operate" like them. He admits falling into this trap himself. "I've had to be very careful to address it head on," he says.

Create a personal learning list

Spend time reading and learning about the experience of underrepresented communities at work. Among the books I recommend are *So You Want to Talk About Race* by Ijeoma Oluo, *White Fragility* by Robin DiAngelo, and *What Works* by Iris Bohnet.[2] I've found Harvard Business Review's *Women at Work* podcast to be an excellent resource as well.

Seek out resources that you wouldn't normally come across and look for books and articles from underrepresented communities. In the United States, that might mean books that include the perspectives of immigrants, people with disabilities, and native American and Indigenous communities.

Not only will this activity help you uncover the biases you're bringing to hiring decisions, it will also equip you with the framework and language to recognize, and possibly call out, bias in your company's processes.

Ask: "Where is bias showing up in this decision, or where could it?"

One team I work with had hiring managers who would often flippantly say things like: "This candidate is qualified, but really isn't a cultural fit." Or "We should hire *this* person. I could easily see myself having a beer with them after work."

These comments, laden with bias, would go unchecked. When the leadership team, which was entirely male and white, asked for my help in creating guidelines to reduce bias in the hiring processes, I suggested they start candidate debrief meetings by asking, "Where could bias show up in our decisions today?" This intervention, along with other process changes, led the team to hire two women leaders.

Explicitly acknowledging that we all have biases, especially unconsciously, and creating a space to call them out forges an opportunity to hold ourselves and each other accountable.

Reduce the influence of your peers' opinions on your hiring decisions

In the past, Microsoft would allow hiring managers to see each other's feedback on a candidate before it was their turn to interview them. "Everybody on the interview loop could see what others were ," says Edward. "It's very clear how that could lead to biases and being influenced by someone else's views."

Recently, the company made the feedback loop private—a hiring manager can't log in to the tool and see their colleagues' feedback until they've entered their own assessment. Edward says that the change has allowed people the freedom to form their own opinions without being influenced by their peers—or their bosses.

Even if you don't use a software tool for hiring loops, refrain from comparing notes verbally until you have formed your own point of view. I recommend writing down your feedback and whether you're inclined to hire the candidate before you debrief with your colleagues. Again, ask yourself as you're writing: "How could bias have impacted my assessment and recommendation?"

Use a "flip it to test" approach

In 2017, *Fortune* 500 executive Kristen Pressner gave a brave TEDx Talk, where she admitted to harboring gender bias against women leaders, despite identifying as a woman herself. Pressner developed a technique to disrupt bias: Ask yourself, if you were to swap out the candidate from a historically unseen background with one of your more typical hires, would you have the same reaction? For example, if a woman of color candidate speaks passionately, and you're less inclined to hire her because you think of her as "angry," would you use the same word if a white man spoke the same way?

"Flip it to test it" is a relatively easy way to call out bias as it happens. In a recent hiring decision that I was part of, a highly qualified woman of color was approached to apply formally for a role for which she was already in-formally performing the duties. Since the organization was already familiar with her work and performance, the hiring manager saw no harm in having her skip the early parts of the hiring process. But some colleagues expressed concern about "bending the rules" for her. During the discussion, I flipped the concern by asking two questions: "Would we have the same reservations if we were circumventing the traditional hiring process for a white person?" and "In the past, when all the candidates we were considering were white men, did we focus extensively on the fairness of the hiring process?" In both cases, the hiring committee unanimously answered no. We were able to recognize our bias and eventually made an offer to the candidate.

Understand how reducing bias could personally benefit you

Diversity in our workplace makes us smarter, more innovative, and promotes better critical thinking.[3] It's not only the organization that benefits; we personally have a lot to gain by working with people from all different backgrounds. By recognizing how we benefit from reducing our own bias—rather than focusing on the ROI for the company—we're likely to be more motivated to take action.

As Michelle Gadsen-Williams, managing director and global head of diversity, equity, and inclusion at Black-Rock, told me, "A culture of equality is a multiplier. We can't achieve a culture of equality if personal unconscious bias is not addressed first and foremost."

Author's note (7/16/20): I updated the language in this article because I am no longer using "diverse" to refer to a person or people. When we categorize people of color or women as "diverse," we are centering white people and men as the accepted norm. I also updated "unconscious bias" to simply be "bias."

———————

Ruchika T. Malhotra is the author of the book *Inclusion on Purpose: An Intersectional Approach to Creating a Culture of Belonging at Work*. She is also the founder of Candour, an inclusion strategy firm. Ruchika is working on her next book, *Uncompete: Dismantling a Competition Mindset to Unlock Liberation, Opportunity, and Peace.*

THREE BEHAVIORAL NUDGES TO REDUCE BIAS IN HIRING

by Paola Cecchi-Dimeglio

Everyone who has worked to get diversity right knows there is no elixir that increases diverse talent. Doing DEI by the numbers just won't get you there. But here's some good news: By focusing on decision intelligence and evidence-based solutions that drive scalable change and boost inclusion, leaders *can* increase the number of diverse candidates that they hire.[a]

As an academic, I've long studied the problem of increasing employee diversity in companies; and as a consultant, I've applied what I've learned to help

(continued)

THREE BEHAVIORAL NUDGES TO REDUCE BIAS IN HIRING

companies hire and promote more fairly. Through this work, I've identified a few behavioral nudges that together form an effective, well-rounded approach— one that can help executives make better, less-biased decisions in hiring.

Generate ranked criteria for candidates

Recruitment can be overwhelming for both interviewers and candidates, but a strategic approach can help bring order to the process. According to decision research, having a solid list of predetermined, prioritized qualifications for a position is key to choosing wisely.[b] The hiring committee should agree on five to 10 qualifications, which may span both technical skills and business acumen, and rank them by importance.

During interviews, the goal is for each qualification and candidate to stand on their own, to shield any assessment from prior influences. After the interview, the interviewer can assign a high, medium, or low rating. For example, in hiring for a communications manager, writing and collaboration might be ranked as the two top skills necessary, while web design might be ranked as fifth or sixth. Then, when assessing the group of candidates, those who scored high on more important factors would end up ranked higher than those who scored high on less-prioritized qualifications, thus surfacing those candidates who exhibited the most important skills for the job. This practice forces assessors to focus separately on each area and score it individually, as opposed to, say, judging the interview to be a total success based on one or two positive elements that may or may not be core to the job.

Creating clear, succinct lists of qualifications provides a set of focal points that can steer decision makers away from race, gender, and socioeconomic background. This strategy should generate diverse sets of options and can be used with a broad range of position types.

Challenge yourself to support the opposite opinion

First interviewed, first hired. Research reveals a tendency to favor early options and undervalue contradictory evidence that comes later.[c] In other words, if you've made an initial judgment, you are more likely to ignore or discount new data that doesn't support it.

An HR professional at a global professional services firm I worked with noticed that 89% of new hires were the first candidates seen. The committee wanted to counter this biasing tendency, so decision makers applied a "thinking of the opposite" strategy. For each candidate who had been favored, the decision makers were challenged to think of reasons why these top candidates might be the *wrong* choice. Similarly, for the

(*continued*)

THREE BEHAVIORAL NUDGES TO REDUCE BIAS IN HIRING

candidates who were not ranked highly, decision makers were challenged to develop an argument for why they might be the *right* fit. When challenged to create the necessary counterarguments, decision makers may go back and refer to data that they initially discounted, ultimately making their decisions more informed and objective.

Modify the environment

Different environments can improve or support high-quality decision-making and impact organizations' hiring efforts. Seemingly small factors such as time slots, room arrangements, and room temperature can all exert influence on the decision-making process.

We can all be choice architects. Choice architecture refers to the way alternatives are presented to decision-makers. For example, one design choice is timing: If you ask someone to rate a candidate before lunch, when they're hungry, their ratings are likely to be harsher.[d] However, if you ask them to do it at a time of day when people tend to have more brainpower and are more relaxed—for example, in the morning—their ratings are likely to be more favorable.

Shifting interview times is one way to use psychological principles to influence behavior for good, so create blocks of time in your calendar when you predict you will be feeling more relaxed and energetic, and allocate that time to rate candidates. To be even more confident in your decision, make an initial decision early in the week and revisit it toward the end of the week. At that point, ask yourself: *Has your thinking evolved, or do you still feel the same way about the decision?*

a. Bruce Posner, "Why You Decide the Way You Do," *MIT Sloan Management Review*, December 16, 2014, https://sloanreview.mit.edu/article/why-you-decide-the-way-you-do/.

b. Ralph L. Keeney, "Value-Focused Brainstorming," *Decision Analysis* 9, no. 4 (December 1, 2012): 303–313, https://doi.org/10.1287/deca.1120.0251.

c. Asher Koriat, Sarah Lichtenstein, and Baruch Fischhoff, "Reasons for Confidence," *Journal of Experimental Psychology: Human Learning and Memory* 6, no. 2 (1980): 107–118, https://doi.org/10.1037/0278-7393.6.2.107.

d. Shai Danziger, Jonathan Levav, and Liora Avnaim-Pesso, "Extraneous Factors in Judicial Decisions,"*PNAS* 108, no. 17 (2011): 6889–6892, https://doi.org/10.1073/pnas.1018033108.

Paola Cecchi-Dimeglio is the chair of the Executive Leadership Research Initiative for Women and Minority Attorneys at Harvard Law School, and a senior research fellow with a joint appointment at Harvard Law School and the Harvard Kennedy School. She is the author of *Diversity Dividend* and the founder of the decision-making consulting firm People Culture Data Consulting Group.

Adapted from "6 Behavioral Nudges to Reduce Bias in Hiring and Promotions" on hbr.org, November 2, 2022 (product #H07BP0).

NOTES

1. Helen Turnbull, PhD, "The Affinity Bias Conundrum: The Illusion of Inclusion—Part III" *Diversity Journal*, May 20, 2014, https://diversityjournal.com/13763-affinity-bias-conundrum-illusion -inclusion-part-iii/.

2. Ijeoma Oluo, *So You Want to Talk About Race* (New York: Seal Press, 2018); Robin J. DiAngelo, *White Fragility: Why It's So Hard for White People to Talk About Racism* (Boston: Beacon Press, 2018); Iris Bohnet, *What Works: Gender Equality by Design* (Cambridge, MA: The Belknap Press of Harvard University Press, 2016).

3. Katherine W. Phillips, "How Diversity Makes Us Smarter," *Greater Good Magazine*, September 18, 2017, https://greatergood. berkeley.edu/article/item/how_diversity_makes_us_smarter.

Attract and Build a Wide Pool of Candidates

SECTION TWO

**Attract
and Build a
Wide Pool of
Candidates**

CHAPTER 7

Don't Post That Job Listing Before Taking These Five Steps

by Marlo Lyons

In the rush to fill positions, many hiring managers often overlook critical steps when scaling their teams. Without conducting a thorough team assessment before creating job descriptions, they risk ending up with skill gaps. Rather than simply adding headcount, it's essential to take a more strategic approach, understanding which additional skill sets and capabilities will truly add value to the team and organization—both now and in the future.

Adapted from content posted on hbr.org, June 4, 2024 (product #H088XW).

Here's how to conduct a comprehensive assessment before creating that job description.

Step 1: Strategically align goals

Begin by aligning your team's goals with organizational objectives. While this may seem obvious, it helps you anticipate evolving skill requirements, ensuring that you hire talent that not only meets current demands but also fuels future agility and growth.

For example, imagine your company is moving toward data-driven marketing but isn't quite there yet. That strategic direction will likely require employees to have skills like data analysis and strategic thinking, as well as technical proficiency in digital marketing platforms, social media analytics, and marketing automation tools. Therefore, a marketing leader will want to seek candidates who can demonstrate deep technical skills as well as marketing skills.

Communicate transparently with candidates about future skill needs to ensure that they won't feel underutilized if all their skills can't be leveraged immediately upon hire.

> **Outcome:** Prevents skills mismatches and will ensure the organization is prepared for evolving demands.

> **Who should be involved:** Your leadership team (or entire team if you have a small team), cross-functional stakeholders, and your manager.

> **Rough time frame:** One to two weeks.

Step 2: Conduct talent planning

Conduct a thorough talent assessment to identify both your whole team's and individual members' existing skills and potential gaps.

Individual skills inventories and tools—for example, the 9Box performance assessment, 360-degree assessments, individual development plans, and talent performance reviews—can help you evaluate each team member's hard and soft skills. This can provide deep insight into which skills and capabilities are missing on your team. Without these insights, you may default to repurposing positions held by long-term employees who lack the skill sets needed for the future but have historical knowledge critical for business continuity.

A SWOT analysis (strengths, weaknesses, opportunities, and threats) can help you identify where your team has excelled and where it has faced challenges while working on previous projects, cross-functional engagements, or organizational changes. Ask cross-functional stakeholders to weigh in on your assessment to ensure that a new hire will fill team gaps in alignment with stakeholders' needs.

Outcome: Ensures your team is skilled and well-equipped to meet current and future challenges, enhancing overall business continuity.

Who should be involved: Your HR partner, your leadership team, and your manager.

Rough time frame: One to two weeks. This can be done concurrently with Step 1.

Step 3: Evaluate team structure

Analyzing the current team structure will help you determine how well it supports your strategic goals and whether existing roles and responsibilities are aligned with the team's objectives. Identify any structural issues that could be addressed by new hires or internal adjustments.

For example, if all of your team managers are considered inexperienced at people leadership, you'll want to hire someone with deep management expertise who can help mentor the novice managers. If your team has work spread across numerous people, thus hampering decision-making, perhaps work needs to be consolidated under one leader, and you may need to hire someone to manage areas that won't be consolidated.

> **Outcome:** Enhances team effectiveness and engagement with an explanation of what hole the new hire will fill.

> **Who should be involved:** Your HR partner and your manager. If you have a large organization, include your leadership team as well.

> **Rough time frame:** Depending on the depth of the organization and its complexity, this could take one month or longer.

Step 4: Identify team cultural nuances

While subject matter expertise, diversity of thought, and technical skills are crucial, ensuring that a candidate can integrate well into the current team will help maintain a harmonious work environment and prevent conflict. Assess your team's unique dynamic to identify which types of personalities have blended into the team well and which have struggled to fit in or be successful. Looking for candidates who can complement the existing team will ensure smooth onboarding and enhance the team's productivity. For example, if your team values close collaboration, a candidate who prefers to work completely independently might create friction that detracts from the work goals.

> **Outcome:** Ensures new hires will seamlessly integrate into team dynamics, leading to smoother onboarding, enhanced collaboration, and increased overall team productivity.

> **Who should be involved:** Your HR partner, your leadership team, and your manager.

> **Rough time frame:** One week.

Step 5: Understand team members' aspirations

This is an overlooked yet critical step before putting together a job description. Employees are more engaged and productive when their aspirations and interests are considered alongside organizational needs. By understanding current team members' values and career interests, leaders can avoid courting new hires with overlapping goals or career interests.

For example, if a leader already has three team members who aspire to manage people, hiring another person with similar ambitions may lead to frustration for them, as they may see themselves as behind the three other tenured team members in line for management opportunities. Conversely, if a seasoned people leader is hired, the three tenured employees may feel they have no room for advancement.

> **Outcome:** Ensures talent development and prevents hiring overlapping skills, thereby reducing potential competition or conflict within the team.

> **Who should be involved:** Your HR partner, your manager, your leadership team for large teams, and for teams over 200 people, consider including the data analytics team to develop a detailed survey.

> **Rough time frame:** This depends on team size—for a small team (up to 10 members), this process may take one to two weeks. For larger teams, it could extend to three to four weeks to hold individual meetings, conduct follow-ups as necessary, and complete analysis of the data.

By embracing a strategic and holistic approach to talent assessment before hiring new employees, companies will be able to uncover additional avenues for growth, optimize team dynamics, and ensure that they bring on board individuals whose capabilities align with the organization's future needs. Ultimately, this proactive approach not only bolsters team effectiveness but also fortifies the organization's resilience by future-proofing its workforce against evolving challenges and opportunities.

———————

Marlo Lyons is a career, executive, and team coach, as well as the award-winning author of *Wanted—A New Career: The Definitive Playbook for Transitioning to a New Career or Finding Your Dream Job*. You can reach her at marlolyonscoaching.com.

CHAPTER 8

Write a Job Description That Attracts the Right Candidate

by Whitney Johnson

Far too many organizations miss golden opportunities to bring onboard the best possible talent for the tasks at hand—and those of the future. When it's time to recruit, hire, and onboard, the most common approaches are routine and rote, prone to misjudgment and error. The process is costly and, in the end, unfruitful.

This failure begins early in the process from when the role is conceived to trying to capture it in a written

---

Adapted from content posted on hbr.org, March 30, 2020 (product #H05HTC).

job description. As international talent management expert Dorothy Dalton laments, "Copy-paste recruitment is generally business as usual in most organizations. . . . Even if the post was last filled five years ago, the chance of anyone thinking it might have to be crafted differently are slim. Generally, the only changes I see are to inflate the qualifications."[1]

If you think the job you're hiring for hasn't changed in the last five years—or even in the past year—then it's probably just about the only thing in your organization that hasn't. And the practice of overinflation of job qualifications often discourages desirable candidates from applying—candidates with potential who won't be easily bored in the role.[2] So instead of leaning on this approach, learn to pinpoint what you really need from a new hire to properly compose and position the job description. Here are four suggestions:

Know what you need now, but also envision the future

Think of the job as an S curve, with lots of room to grow in the role at the low end of the "S" and high proficiency but little potential at the top end. In most cases, I advocate hiring someone who will onboard at the low end and enjoy an enthusiastic and extended growth experience, with a commensurate level of job engagement, satisfaction, and productivity as they ascend the curve to reach high proficiency.

Sometimes, however, you need a sharpshooter with the expertise to solve a pressing problem. You can't wait for them to grow. The trade-off is that they will quickly move on, either to another organization or to a new challenge in yours (if one is available for them), and you will need to hire again, hopefully for a longer tenure.

Before writing the job description, think about what will best serve the organization in both the short and long term. In some cases, it may be more appropriate to contract a gig worker to solve the problem and hire an employee for longer-term growth.

Understand the hiring context

Evaluate the role in the context of the team in a large organization, or in the whole organization if your workplace is on the smaller side. Filling a job is a growth opportunity for the business, not just for the individual; the best fit is found when it captures growth for both. You can better align your job openings and descriptions with what your business needs by better understanding your current roles.

For example, we consulted with a company that had motivated midlevel managers who were nonetheless uncertain about opportunities for advancement. This was especially true for people who had worked in the organization for more than 10 years. As the company developed new jobs to be filled, we recommended that it survey a targeted group of individuals related to the role they were hiring for. In the survey, they asked people to outline what they actually did versus the job description for their role. Questions included: *Why do these differences exist? What has motivated or required them to do things differently than their job description would suggest? What tasks are associated with the standard phrase "and other jobs as specified?" What challenges have they faced and overcome to be successful? How is success gauged— what are the metrics used?* And, finally, *How long have they been in this role?*

This type of survey can identify roles that need to be trimmed or pruned out altogether. Results can facilitate proper allocation of valuable human resources and help identify opportunities for internal movement and advancement of proven talent. You may even find you don't need an external hire at all, or that you need to hire for something different than the vacant position. Ultimately, you will be properly informed when writing the job description if you know what current employees are doing and what they *want* to be doing. The gaps will reveal themselves.

Avoid limiting language

As I noted earlier, the goal of a job description is to invite applicants. To do this successfully, avoid limiting language. Gender-biased language, for example, is known to discourage possible candidates, so avoid words that have overly masculine or feminine connotations (such as "competitive" or "nurturing").[3]

Similarly, careless language can discourage applicants who are not white, who are "young" or "old" (adding quotes because perceptions of age can vary by individuals, cultures, industries, and the like), or whom have unconventional career paths (such as gig workers, on-rampers, or late-career folks). Avoid using terms like "career-oriented" or "experienced" or "energetic" to widen the pool of candidates you appeal to. If you're trying to diversify your workforce (and I hope you are) then include language specifically inviting diverse interest. Kristen Pressner, the global head of human resources for Roche Diagnostics, advocates that we "flip it to test" our language:[4] If you're a man, how might your language sound to a woman? If you're white, how might the job description read for a person of color? If you're a driven career person, would what you've crafted invite an applicant who needs to work from home? Also test the language you use with a diverse group of individuals before you post. They can help illuminate your blind spots.

Think about meaning

People want to contribute, to feel energized and passionate about what they do. They want to be inspired by ideas that can help solve problems and meet needs. This doesn't necessarily mean changing the world or addressing cosmically important issues. But it does mean believing that we are making our corner of the world happier, brighter, and safer in some small but significant way.

It is critical that organizations ensure that the roles they are hiring for are quality opportunities for meaningful work, personal growth, and impact. This needs to be conveyed through the job description and even into the interviewing process. For example, Chatbooks is a company that helps people create printed scrapbooks from their Instagram photos. Rather than focusing on specific skills, they use words like "high-performance creativity," "grown up," and "optimistic" to describe their values and the kind of candidates they are seeking to employ. When you hire an individual whose values align with the purposes of your organization, it's a win-win. Craft the job description to invite those people to apply.

When you get a job description right, you provide an opportunity for your next employee to assume market risk—to play where others in your organization aren't, utilizing their distinctive strengths. The odds of success are much higher than if they face competitive risk, battling for turf with entrenched players. The right fit means that a new hire has room to grow. And when your employees grow, so does your organization.

———————

Whitney Johnson is the CEO of Disruption Advisors, a change management advisory firm, and the author of *Smart Growth: How to Grow Your People to Grow Your Company.*

NOTES

1. Dorothy Dalton, "Why Copy-Paste Recruitment Fails in Today's Market," dorothydalton.com, February 5, 2016, https://dorothydalton.com/2016/02/25/why-copy-paste-recruitment-fails/?utm_source=ReviveOldPost&utm_medium=social&utm_campaign=ReviveOldPost.

2. Whitney Johnson, "If You Are Looking to Hire (or Get Hired), Here Are Some Things to Consider," LinkedIn, January 23, 2019, https://www.linkedin.com/pulse/you-looking-hire-get-hired-here-some-things-consider-whitney-johnson/.

3. Rachel Blakely-Gray, "Is Gender-Biased Language Creeping into Your Job Descriptions?" Top Echelon, February 1, 2019, https://topechelon.com/blog/gender-biased-language-in-job-descriptions/.

4. Janine Milne, "'Flip It to Test It': Lessons on Battling Bias from Roche," diginomica, March 18, 2018, https://diginomica.com/flip-it-to-test-it-lessons-on-battling-bias-from-roche.

Conduct Effective Interviews

CHAPTER 9

How to Conduct an Effective Interview

by Rebecca Knight

The virtual stack of résumés in your inbox is winnowed, and certain candidates have passed the initial screen. Next step: interviews. How should you use the relatively brief time to get to know—and assess—a near stranger? How many people at your firm should be involved? How can you tell if a candidate will be a good fit? And finally, should you really ask questions like: "What's your greatest weakness?"

What the Experts Say

Hiring the right person for a job has become increasingly difficult, regardless of shifting labor market conditions.

Adapted from "How to Conduct an Effective Job Interview" on hbr.org, January 23, 2015 (product #H01U97).

"Pipelines are depleted and more companies are competing for top talent," says Claudio Fernández-Aráoz, a former partner and member of the executive committee of the global executive search firm Egon Zehnder and author of *It's Not the How or the What but the Who: Succeed by Surrounding Yourself with the Best*. Applicants have more information about each company's selection process than ever before. Career websites like Glassdoor have taken the "mystique and mystery" out of interviews, says John Sullivan, an HR expert, professor of management at San Francisco State University, and author of *1000 Ways to Recruit Top Talent*. If your organization's interview process turns candidates off, "they will roll their eyes and find other opportunities," even in a tough labor market, he warns. Your job is to assess candidates but also to convince the best ones to stay. Here's how to make the interview process work for you—and for them.

Prepare your questions

Before you meet candidates, you need to figure out exactly what you're looking for in a new hire so that you're asking the right questions during the interview. Begin this process by "compiling a list of required attributes" for the position and asking "In which ways do we want to change our culture?" suggests Fernández-Aráoz. For inspiration and guidance, Sullivan recommends looking at your top performers. What do they have in common? What skills are missing? How are they resourceful? What did they accomplish prior to working at your organization? What roles did they hold? Those answers will help you create criteria and enable you to construct relevant questions.

Reduce stress

Candidates find job interviews stressful because of the many unknowns: *What will my interviewer be like? What kinds of questions will they ask? How can I squeeze this meeting into my workday?* And of course: *What should I wear?* But "when people are stressed, they do not perform as well," says Sullivan. He recommends taking preemptive steps to lower the candidate's cortisol levels. Tell people in advance the topics you'd like to discuss so they can prepare. Be willing to meet the person at a time that's convenient to them. And explain your organization's dress code. Your goal is to "make them comfortable" so that you have a productive, professional conversation.

Involve (only a few) others

When making any big decision, it's important to seek counsel from others so invite a few trusted colleagues to help you interview. "Monarchy doesn't work. You want to have multiple checks" to make sure you hire the right person, Fernández-Aráoz explains. "But on the other hand, extreme democracy is also ineffective" and can result in a long-drawn-out process which increases the chances of rejecting or losing the right candidates for the wrong reasons. He recommends having three people interview the candidate: "the boss, the boss's boss, and a senior HR person or recruiter." Peer interviewers can also be "really important," Sullivan observes, because they give your team members a say in who gets the job. He adds, "They will take more ownership of the hire and have reasons to help that person succeed."

Assess potential

Budget 90 minutes for the first interview, says Fernández-Aráoz. That amount of time enables you to "really assess the person's competency and potential." Look for signs of the candidate's "curiosity, insight, engagement, and determination." Sullivan advises interviewers to "assume that the person will be promoted and that they will be a manager someday. The question then becomes not only 'Can this person do the job today?' but 'Can they do the job a year from now when the world has changed?'" Ask the candidate how they learn and for their thoughts on where your industry is going. "No one can predict the future, but you want someone who is thinking about it every day," he explains.

Ask for real solutions

Don't waste your breath with absurd questions like: *What are your weaknesses?* "You might as well say, 'Lie to me,'" says Sullivan. Instead try to discern how the candidate would handle real situations related to the job. Explain a problem your team struggles with and ask the candidate to walk you through how they would solve it. Or describe a process your company uses and ask the candidate to identify inefficiencies. Go back to your list of desired attributes, says Fernández-Aráoz. If you're looking for an executive who will need to influence a large number of people over whom they won't have formal power, ask: "Have you ever been in a situation where you had to persuade other people who were not your direct reports to do something? How did you do it? And what were the consequences?"

Consider "cultural fit," but don't obsess

Much has been made about the importance of "cultural fit" in successful hiring. And you should look for signs that "the candidate will be comfortable" at your organization, says Fernández-Aráoz. Think about your company's work environment and compare it to the candidate's orientation. Are they a long-term planner or a short-term thinker? Are they collaborative or do they prefer working independently? But, says Sullivan, your perception of a candidate's disposition isn't necessarily indicative of whether they can acclimate to a new culture. "People adapt," he says. "What you really want to know is: Can they adjust?"

Sell the job

If the meeting is going well and you believe that the candidate is worth wooing, spend time during the second half of the interview selling the role and the organization. "If you focus too much on selling at the beginning, it's hard to be objective," says Fernández-Aráoz. But once you're confident in the candidate, "tell the person why you think they are a good fit." Bear in mind that the interview is a mutual screening process. "Make the process fun," says Sullivan. Ask them if there's anyone on the team they'd like to meet. The best people to sell the job are those who "live it," he explains. "Peers give an honest picture of what the organization is like."

Case Study: Provide Relevant, Real-Life Scenarios to Reveal How Candidates Think

The vast majority of hires at Four Kitchens, a web design firm in Austin, Texas, are through employee referrals. So when Todd Ross Nienkerk, the company's cofounder and CEO, had an opening for an account manager, he had a hunch about who should get the job. "It was somebody who'd been a finalist for a position here years ago," says Todd. (We'll call her Deborah.) "We kept her in mind, and when this job opened, she was the first person we called."

Even though Deborah was a favored candidate, she again went through the company's three-step interview process. The first focused on skills. When Four Kitchens interviews designers or coders, it typically asks applicants to provide a portfolio of work. "We ask them to talk us through their process. We're not grilling them, but we want to know how they think, and we want to see their personal communication style." But for the account manager role, Todd took a slightly different tack. Before the interview, he and the company's head of business development put together a job description and then came up with questions based on the relevant responsibilities. They started with questions like: *What are things you look for in a good client? What are red flags in a client relationship? How do you deal with stress?*

Then Todd presented Deborah with a series of redacted client emails that represented a cross-section of day-to-day communication: Some were standard requests for status updates; others involved serious contract disputes and pointed questions. "We said, 'Pretend you work here. Talk us through how you'd handle this.' It put her on the spot, but frankly, this is what the job entails."

After a successful first round, Deborah moved on to the second phase, the team interview. In this instance, she met with a project manager, a designer, and two developers. "These are an opportunity for applicants to find out what it's like to work here," says Todd. "But the biggest reason we do it is to ensure that everyone is involved in the process and feels a sense of ownership over the hire."

The final stage was the partner interview, during which Todd asked Deborah questions about career goals and the industry. "It was also an opportunity for her to ask us tough questions about where our company is headed," he says.

Deborah got the job.

———————

Rebecca Knight is a journalist who writes about all things related to the changing nature of careers and the workplace. Her essays and reported stories have been featured in the *Boston Globe*, *Business Insider*, the *New York Times*, BBC, and the *Christian Science Monitor*. She was shortlisted as a Reuters Institute Fellow at Oxford University in 2023. Earlier in her career, she spent a decade as an editor and reporter at the *Financial Times* in New York, London, and Boston.

CHAPTER 10

Evaluate a Candidate's Critical Thinking Skills

by Christopher Frank, Paul Magnone, and Oded Netzer

Hiring is one of the most challenging competencies to master, yet it is one of the most strategic and impactful managerial functions. A McKinsey study quantified that superior talent is up to eight times more productive, showing that the relationship between talent quality and business performance is dramatic.[1] Organizations

Adapted from "How to Evaluate a Job Candidate's Critical Thinking Skills in an Interview" on hbr.org, September 25, 2023 (product #H07T10).

seeking growth or simply survival during difficult times must successfully recruit A-list talent, thought leaders, and subject matter experts. This is often done under time constraints, as they must quickly fill a key position. Essentially, you are committing to a long-term relationship after a few very short dates.

Now let's consider the typical process of hiring talent. The primary tool we use to assess talent is a set of job interviews. The typical interview process is a Q&A format where some version of the common questions are asked of the candidate: *Tell us about your background. Why do you want to work for us? Share a challenge you faced at work and how you dealt with it. What are you most proud of? What impact have you had? Why are you the best person for the job? What is your greatest achievement? What are your weaknesses?*

While much has been said in favor and against the value of interviews themselves, the typical Q&A job interview process fails to assess one of the most important, if not *the* most important, skills you should be looking for from people you hire—critical thinking. Critical thinking is seeking information from various sources, assessing its credibility, and determining its relevance and veracity. Often classified as a higher-order skill, critical thinking is not a single skill but a collection of skills involving reasoning, constructing sound arguments, and identifying a situation's flaws, biases, logic, or inconsistencies. Critical thinking is different from creative thinking. Creative thinking is the ability to generate new, innovative ideas. Critical thinking requires the candidate to seek information by asking questions, carefully and logically analyze facts, and form a judgment.

Critical Thinking Is Fundamentally a Process of Questioning

A key insight from the research for our book *Decisions Over Decimals*, based on surveying and teaching thousands of executives, is that the smartest person in the room is not the one with the answer but the person asking the question. They are curious, engaged, unafraid, inquisitive, and ready to explore a new domain that may not have answers yet. By the nature of their questions, they demonstrate observation, analysis, inference, interrogation, interpretation, and explanation. Critical thinkers are curious. Innate curiosity has been shown to be associated with the following eight traits—avid learners, problem solvers, active listeners, self-driven, high productivity, growth mindset, overachievers, and strong at stakeholder management. These traits read like a wish list of qualifications for people you want to be part of your team.

Consulting firms and technology companies have pushed the standard battery of interview questions by using scenario-based or behavioral questions*: How much should you charge to mow a lawn in Atlanta? Why are utility holes round? How would you design a wine rack for people who are blind? If you received $5 million to solve a global problem, what issue would you address and how?*

These are a good step forward, but while answers to these questions will give you a good idea of candidates' problem-solving skills, ability to deal with ambiguity, and creative thinking, they will not indicate if the candidates are curious, self-starters, or passionate about your company, products, culture, or any of the eight traits referenced earlier.

How do you identify individuals with this versatile and compelling mix of critical thinking and curiosity? Boldly *flip the interview process*.

The oldest and still the most powerful tactic for fostering critical thinking is the Socratic method, developed over 2,400 years ago by the Greek philosopher Socrates. The Socratic method uses thought-provoking question-and-answer probing to promote learning. It focuses on generating more questions than answers, where the answers are not a stopping point but the beginning of further analysis. Hiring managers can apply this model to create a different dialogue with candidates in a modern organization.

The Flip Interview

Let the candidate interview you. The flip interview is an alternate method to uncover a candidate's intrinsic strengths, preferred ways of working, and how they think. The interview will showcase the candidate's thinking and decision-making process and indicate if the candidate exhibits leadership traits.

The flip interview goes beyond letting the candidate ask you open-ended questions like, "What is the company culture?" or "What is it like to work for the company?" The interviewer comes to the discussion with a business scenario, an understanding of relevant information, and an invitation to the interviewee to guide discovery through a series of questions.

The interviewee may use four types of questions, listed below by increasing level of complexity and involvement.

- **Factual questions:** Questions that have straight-forward answers based on facts or awareness.

- **Convergent questions:** Close-ended questions with finite answers. Typically, these questions have one correct answer.

- **Divergent questions:** Open-ended questions that encourage many answers. These questions are a means for analyzing a situation, problem, or complexity in greater detail and stimulate creative thought.

- **Evaluative questions:** Questions that require deeper levels of thinking. They can be open or closed. Evaluative questions elicit analysis at multiple levels and from different perspectives to arrive at newly synthesized information or conclusions.

Conducting the Flip Interview: A Four-Step Process

Use the following framework to maximize the value of your conversations with recruits:

1. Frame

Briefly describe a scenario. State up front that you are the source of information for the scenario and ask the interviewee to drive the next eight to 12 minutes with a straightforward "How would you start this discovery?" When they inevitably get stuck, prompt them with a branch of the decision tree that opens the discovery further. Invite them to ask questions.

Interviewer evaluation:

In the framing step, you evaluate how they frame the problem. Do they take the situation at face value or probe to get at the essence of the situation? The quality of the questions they ask should lead to determining the information they need, the effort required, and uncover the essential decision to be made. This first step is all about problem-finding more than problem-solving.

2. Link

Once they define the problem, invite them to ask questions about context: "Given how you framed the scenario, what other information would you like to know to work toward a recommendation?"

Interviewer evaluation:

You are looking to see if their questions lead them to put the scenario in context. Understanding the context is crucial. To truly put a situation in context, their questions should enable them to triangulate it by looking at it in (1) absolute terms, (2) over time, and (3) relative to what's going on across the market, with customers or actions from competitors.

3. Interrogate

Based on the original scenario, combined with what they learned, ask, "What is the essential decision that is needed?" or "How has their understanding of the situation shifted?"

Interviewer evaluation:

Have they interrogated the situation properly? Are they able to start to formulate the narrative? You are assessing if their narrative is a summary or a synthesis: *summary* is statement of the data; *synthesis* is data plus judgment. The critical thinker will demonstrate how they can consume and synthesize different pieces of information in parallel to arrive at a deeper understanding of the scenario or decision needed.

4. Perform

In this final step, ask, "What are the immediate next steps you would take?"

Interviewer evaluation:

If they start to ask questions about key stakeholders, shadow influencers, advocates, or swing voters who need to be convinced, the candidate is thinking critically. Do they seek to learn about headwinds and tailwinds to enable them to move forward? Note: This is not about solving the problem or assessing if they develop a recommendation, but simply how they approach problem-solving and decisions.

Using a flip interview, you can evaluate the candidate's logic and passion for the role based on their questions. Are the questions superfluous or consequential? Are the questions generic or specific? Do they ask not only factual or convergent but also divergent and evaluative questions? Does the candidate pivot, dive deep, and revisit a topic from different angles? Are the questions grounded in the context of the problem and its environment? As they ask you questions, it will enable you to determine if they are actively listening by adjusting their questions in real-time, pivoting, and probing.

A skilled questioner creates a cooperative dialogue to elicit new learning through a series of questions. They engage the other person. Their questions should lead to inferences and connections and open up viewpoints that are not apparent. This exploration mindset encourages trial and iteration; unexpected learning may originate from the discussion.

Successful candidates in the flip interview will demonstrate a critical thinking mindset. This is different from knowing analytic tools and methods. A critical thinking philosophy is a skill that almost every leader seeks, and many teams have only in short supply. Thinking analytically and critically includes being clear about the purpose of the essential question rather than wandering in the forest of data, being inquisitive not from a statistical perspective but questioning the initial face value, being able to connect the dots via synthesis, and eventually being able to tell an informed story that is based on deeper truths, judgment, and context, not just restating the initial facts.

Reactivity, insight, and ingenuity are needed for companies to thrive. You seek agile thinkers who can be growth champions, truth-tellers, customer stewards, and insight creators. The candidate who can conceptualize the problem, frame the situation, and ask more thoughtful questions will outperform those relying on textbook answers. Hiring talent capable of asking thoughtful questions is the key to building successful teams.

Finally, once you successfully recruit amazing people, you must create an environment where employees are motivated to work collectively yet feel valued and recognized for being curious and inquisitive. An entire organization with a growth mindset that embraces questions and curiosity can reframe challenges as opportunities and move more freely to adjust to business conditions.

Case Study: Microsoft Changes the Interview Process

While their interview was not labeled as a flip interview, a candidate applied for a job at Microsoft in 1998 and found himself in one. During the interview, the recruiter prompted: "Sell me a toaster." The candidate paused. Then they started to ask questions: "How many people are in the family?" "Are there young children in the house?" "What is the age range of toaster users in the family?" "Do they live in a small space, such as an apartment, or a large house?" "Are they big breakfast eaters, or is their main meal dinner?" "How often do they eat out?" For three minutes, it was a stream of questions about demographics, psychographics, and physical space. The recruiter asked the candidate to stop and asked what this had to do with selling a toaster. The candidate replied, "Everything."

It is important to discover and understand the context of the "toaster environment" to ensure I sell you what you need. If I match the toaster features and functions to your needs, the success of the sales increases, and you will be a satisfied customer. Do you need a toaster oven, a pop-up two-slice toaster, a four-slice, a wide-slice toaster, a conveyor toaster, a commercial toaster, or a convection oven? Maybe a panini press would serve your needs best.

The exercise was not about the toaster: The recruiter was looking to see how the candidate handled ambiguity. Were they a critical thinker? Did they dive right in with a sales pitch or pause, learn, and pivot? In case you are wondering, the candidate got the job.

———————————

Christopher Frank is the coauthor of *Decisions Over Decimals: Striking the Balance between Intuition and Information* and *Drinking from the Fire Hose: Making Smarter Decisions Without Drowning in Information.* He has 25 years of experience with Microsoft and American Express. He is the chief client officer at PSB Insights, a WPP company.

Paul Magnone is the coauthor of *Decisions Over Decimals: Striking the Balance between Intuition and Information* and *Drinking from the Fire Hose: Making*

Smarter Decisions Without Drowning in Information. He currently serves as the head of global strategic alliances for Google.

Oded Netzer is the coauthor of *Decisions Over Decimals: Striking the Balance between Intuition and Information.* He is the Vice Dean for Research and the Arthur J. Samberg Professor of Business at Columbia Business School, an affiliate of the Columbia Data Science Institute, and an Amazon Scholar.

NOTE

1. Paolo Benedet and Ivo Nikolov, "Winning the War for Talent in Product Development," McKinsey and Company, February 3, 2022, https://www.mckinsey.com/capabilities/operations/our-insights/operations-blog/winning-the-war-for-talent-in-product-development.

CHAPTER 11

What to Do When You Don't Click with a Candidate

by Rae Ringel

You're 10 minutes into an interview, and it's not going well. The candidate's answers are fine, but they're not sparking your interest. You have at least 35 more minutes allotted together. Don't write them off or muddle through wasting everyone's time by continuing on this path. You have more power than you think to bring life back to a lackluster interview.

It's often easier for hiring managers to connect with candidates who have similar backgrounds, pedigrees, credentials, or perspectives. In fact, research shows that

---

Adapted from "How to Interview a Candidate You Don't Immediately Click With" on hbr.org, March 4, 2024 (product #H081MJ).

implicit bias shapes interviewers' perceptions of candidates in profound ways.[1] At the same time, research also attests to the enormous benefits of diversity.[2] As organizations experiment with new ways to attract and retain underrepresented talent, the job interview dynamic merits further attention.

Fortunately, there are proven strategies for boosting your chances of clicking with an interviewee, no matter how or whether your backgrounds align. Here are some steps to breathe new life into interviews that appear to be at their last gasp.

Move your questions into a different domain

If your questions about a candidate's experience and credentials are being met with stilted or incomplete answers, move into a different domain. Instead of focusing on the past, turn to the future: Where do they see themselves three years from now? How will your organization look, feel, and function differently if they're brought on board? Or venture into the realm of magic wands and hypotheticals: "If you were starting a company tomorrow, what would its top three values be?"

If a conversation about tasks, capabilities, and responsibilities is going nowhere, try pivoting toward interpersonal dynamics, which are key to getting things done in any workplace. This area showcases candidates' emotional intelligence. Conversation starters might include: "Tell me about a workplace conflict you were involved in—how did you manage it?" or "What was a moment of pride you experienced recently?" or "How do you respond when a manager criticizes your work?"

Give them control

Typically, interviews end with a standard question: "Is there anything you'd like to ask me?" This, of course, isn't really an invitation to pose the burning questions that are *really* on a candidate's mind—like "When can I expect to be promoted?" or "Is this actually a great place to work, or is all the talk about culture and work-life balance just lip service?" More often, it's code for, "Here's your chance to dazzle me with a question that makes you look smart and shows that you've done your homework on us."

If an interview is lacking chemistry, consider handing the reins over earlier in the conversation, with an invitation that's more genuine. Perhaps ask the candidate, "What should I be asking you?" or "What question do you wish I had asked?" Being the interviewee can feel powerless. Questions like this disrupt that dynamic and allow the candidate to set the agenda.

Give them a challenge

Some people are uncomfortable talking about themselves for reasons that may stem from personality, culture, or neurodivergence. When they're aware that this is an issue for them, it can compound the problem. They may retreat further inward as their self-consciousness spirals, or they may overcompensate by name-dropping or raising their volume. If you suspect this might be the root of the disconnect, try shifting the focus from the person to the work.

One strategy is to fill the candidate in on a challenge that the team they'd be joining is currently struggling with, and ask what suggestions they have for tackling it. Since the problem is active and ongoing, there's no pressure to come up with the "right" answer. Instead, you'll get a glimpse into how the person thinks, their willingness to explore angles from all sides, the questions they ask, and the creativity they bring. Collaborative problem-solving skills are in high demand, and this can be an opportunity to assess them in action.

Steer them toward career development

Today's candidates prize career development.[3] If your organization is investing in this area, describe some of your career development options to the candidate and ask which ones excite them the most. You can learn a lot about someone by seeing how they approach learning itself. What skills and capabilities are they most eager to cultivate? Are there other offerings they'd like to see on your career development menu?

Career development benefits individuals as well as the organization. When you bring in employees who are invested in learning and growing, their current skill sets are less important than the certainty that they'll evolve alongside the business.

Get curious

Leaders often rise based on their ability to make quick judgments. When it comes to interviewing job candidates, this can be a liability. If you're not connecting with a candidate, resist the temptation to cut things short or check out mentally. Instead, go in the opposite direction. Embrace your curiosity.

You might start by getting curious about why the conversation isn't flowing or the cadence doesn't feel right. Challenge yourself to consider what might be at play: Might the candidate be distracted because they're wearing jeans while you're in a suit, or the other way around? Could this be their first in-person interview after years of remote work—or their first time being assessed remotely? What would happen if you paused for a longer period of time after posing each question, inviting the candidate to take their time answering?

If you're struggling to muster genuine curiosity, double down on *conveying* that you're interested and engaged. Open-ended questions like "What inspires you?" or "What's something that you find interesting but others might find boring?" often elicit new energy, sparking interest that's authentic.

Set the stage for success

There are certain stage-setters that can improve your chances of connecting with an interviewee. If you know you have a tendency to connect more fluidly with people of a certain gender, ethnicity, or educational background, make a quick list of these "affinity biases" so you're more fully aware of your need to work against them.

Give yourself and the candidate time to prepare by making all necessary materials (including topics of discussion or assignments) available ahead of the interview. Slow thinkers can be the deepest thinkers, and this gives them time to gather their thoughts and make their best case.

If you're conducting a remote interview, consider letting candidates choose between a videoconference or phone call. People's home office and technology setups may vary, and it would be a shame if a distracting Zoom background or spotty connection kept you from identifying the best person for the job.

Above all, it's important to remember that recruiters and hiring managers are not just gatekeepers, but ambassadors for their organizations. If you're not clicking with a candidate, chances are they're also not clicking with you.

By working thoughtfully and strategically to move the conversation in a different direction, you'll raise your chances of leaving candidates with a positive impression. At the very least, they'll have good things to say about their candidate experience. And you may just discover an overlooked gem who'd be absolutely perfect for your team.

———————

Rae Ringel is the president of The Ringel Group, a leadership development consultancy specializing in facilitation, coaching, and training. She is a faculty member at the Georgetown University Institute for Transformational Leadership and the founder of the Executive Certificate in Facilitation program.

NOTES

1. Zhiyu Feng, Yukun Liu, Zhen Wang, and Krishna Savani, "Research: A Method for Overcoming Implicit Bias When Considering Job Candidates," hbr.org, July 21, 2020, https://hbr.org/2020/07/research-a-method-for-overcoming-implicit-bias-when-considering-job-candidates.

2. David Michels, Kevin Murphy, and Karthik Venkataraman, "How Investing in DEI Helps Companies Become More Adaptable," hbr.org, May 5, 2023, https://hbr.org/2023/05/how-investing-in-dei -helps-companies-become-more-adaptable.

3. Todd Horst, Kathryn Kuhn, Stephanie Madner, Charlotte Seiler, and Paul Roche, "Cracking the Code On Digital Talent," mckinsey.com, April 20, 2023, https://www.mckinsey.com/industries/technology -media-and-telecommunications/our-insights/cracking-the-code-on -digital-talent.

CHAPTER 12

Make Interviews More Accessible

by Rebecca Knight

Designing an accessible, inclusive interview process for disabled people and people with different learning styles both widens the talent pool and creates a more equitable workplace.

For hiring managers, this requires a thoughtful and conscientious approach. Where do you begin? What actions can you take to accommodate candidates' needs? How do you maintain consistent evaluation criteria? And how can you set up an environment where all candidates have opportunities to demonstrate their strengths?

Adapted from "How to Make Job Interviews More Accessible" on hbr.org, June 7, 2024 (product #H088YP).

What the Experts Say

Disability, as defined by the International Classification of Impairments, Disabilities and Handicaps, refers to "any restriction or lack (resulting from an impairment) of ability to perform an activity in the manner or within the range considered normal for a human being."[1] A record share of disabled people were employed in the United States last year, according to a report from the Bureau of Labor Statistics.[2] This is progress but more can be done, according to Katie Bach, a former nonresident senior fellow at the Brookings Institution who has spent most of her career focused on job creation, access, and quality.

It starts with creating a level playing field in job interviews. "Offering accommodations to candidates is table stakes," she says. "What I see as the next step is not just asking individuals if they need accommodation, but helping candidates think through what kinds of accommodations might be possible."

Reimagining old, outmoded interview tactics is also key, says Ludmila Praslova, professor of organizational psychology at Vanguard University and the author of *The Canary Code: A Guide to Neurodiversity, Dignity, and Intersectional Belonging at Work*.[3] "We've been using the same methods for years without considering what's truly needed for a specific job and how to identify the right candidate," she says. After all, the goal of job interviews is to uncover a candidate's potential and "assess whether that individual has the necessary skills for the role; everything else creates unnecessary barriers."

Here are some strategies for making your job interviews fairer and more inclusive.

Increase your understanding of disability

First things first: You need to break free from your preconceived ideas about disability, says Bach. "Many of us hold a certain image of what disability looks like and assume that we haven't worked with many disabled people."

But statistically speaking, this belief is unlikely to reflect reality. Roughly one in four Americans lives with a disability, according to the Centers for Disease Control and Prevention, and studies suggest that about 9% of Americans have a learning difference.[4] Many of these differences and disabilities are hidden or invisible.

Meanwhile, 61% of disabled workers have experienced bias, mistreatment, and bullying on the job, research shows.[5] "Once you broaden your understanding of disability and its implications," says Bach, "you realize it's far more prevalent and complex than you thought."

Which is all to say that when it comes to designing more inclusive, accessible job interviews, "sometimes you need to open yourself up to less comfortable forms of understanding," notes Praslova. "That means listening without judgment and not making assumptions about someone faking or being lazy or high-maintenance."

Recognize that people may need accommodations and that strict conformity to traditional interview methods can perpetuate bias. Empathy is important—but even empathy has its limitations, Praslova observes: "It's not about you, it's about the other person. And their reality might be very different from yours."

Look critically at your current practices

Next, examine your current interview practices and techniques and identify unnecessary hurdles that don't reflect actual job requirements.

"Sometimes interviews are designed to trick people, make them emotional, and throw them off balance to see how they perform under pressure," says Praslova. But these tactics could disproportionately disadvantage candidates with social anxiety or neurodivergent thinking, and thus pose greater challenges in these situations. "You're not interviewing for the Secret Service," she says.

Bach agrees. The interview doesn't have to perfectly mimic the conditions of the job, but you might want to examine any "physically and psychologically demanding practices" and perhaps make adjustments, she says. (More on this later.) Do interviews need to be all-day marathons? Must they include 90-minute-long, on-the-fly case studies? Do they even need to be in person? "If it's not part of the job, you need to ask yourself: 'Are we creating an environment that anyone can thrive in? Or are we making it artificially hard?'"

Ask candidates what they need

Unfortunately, there isn't a one-size-fits-all solution for making interviews more inclusive, says Bach. "Even people with the same disability can have different symptoms and severities," which is why you need to work with individual candidates to determine what they might need.

Bach suggests creating "a menu of possible accommodations" that includes examples of what's been done in the past. This might include providing extra time for completing tasks or responding to interview questions, presenting questions in different formats to address different learning styles, or conducting remote interviews for candidates who may have mobility challenges.

Praslova recommends sharing this menu of options with all candidates and encouraging them to request additional support if needed. "Make it clear that it's safe to ask for things and it won't be held against them," she says, noting research that suggests disclosing a disability at work is often a fraught experience.[6] Praslova champions the "platinum rule"—an evolved version of the golden rule: "Treat others as they want to be treated," she says. "It's not what *you* want, it's what the *other person* wants."

Build in flexibility and humanity

In addition to offering specific accommodations, Praslova suggests building flexibility, convenience, and humanity into your interviews. "If you create environments that are good for canaries, they'll be good for everyone," she says. For example, she recommends conducting interviews in quiet, private spaces to reduce distractions and sensory overload; limiting the number of interviews a candidate must attend in one day; and providing personalized support.

"If you're inviting people to a physical site, meet them at the door and guide them to the interview," she says. "If it's a virtual interview, don't assume [they're familiar and comfortable with the platform your company prefers].

Even when things feel obvious to you, try to put yourself in the candidate's shoes."

Praslova also recommends providing all candidates with interview questions in advance. Not only does this allow them time to prepare thoughtful responses, it also removes some of the psychological stress associated with interviews. Otherwise, she says, you may unintentionally place a higher value on their confidence, rather than their skills and abilities. "When you're measuring people's quickness on their feet, sometimes what you're getting is their overconfidence."

Use structured interviews

While open-ended, more casual interviews have their appeal, research shows that structured interviews—which involve a set number of predetermined questions—are less biased and tend to offer a more accurate assessment of a candidate's suitability for a role.[7] "A lot of interviews basically come down to some variation of the airport test: Does this person vibe with me?" says Praslova. Structured interviews, on the other hand, "have checklists and processes that scaffold hiring managers into fairness."

To ensure fairness and objectivity, evaluate candidates solely on these established criteria and support your assessment with solid evidence. Don't let factors like what the candidate is wearing, how nervous they appear, or how easily they engage in small talk influence the interview, she adds. "Know what you're assessing and only assess that," she says. "Candidates want you to focus on their strengths and abilities and what they can do."

This article follows the preference of autistic and disabled communities for identity-first language.

Rebecca Knight is a journalist who writes about all things related to the changing nature of careers and the workplace. Her essays and reported stories have been featured in the *Boston Globe, Business Insider,* the *New York Times,* BBC, and the *Christian Science Monitor.* She was shortlisted as a Reuters Institute Fellow at Oxford University in 2023. Earlier in her career, she spent a decade as an editor and reporter at the *Financial Times* in New York, London, and Boston.

NOTES

1. Krista L. Best, W. Ben Mortenson, Zach Lauzière-Fitzgerald, and Emma M. Smith, "Language Matters! The Long-Standing Debate Between Identity-First Language and Person-First Language," *Assistive Technology* 34, no. 2 (2022): 127–128, doi:10.1080/10400435 .2022.2058315.

2. "Persons with a Disability: Labor Force Characteristics–2023," US Department of Labor, Bureau of Labor Statistics, February 22, 2024, https://www.bls.gov/news.release/pdf/disabl.pdf.

3. Ludmila N. Praslova, PhD, *The Canary Code: A Guide to Neurodiversity, Dignity, and Intersectional Belonging at Work* (Oakland, CA: Berrett-Koehler Publishers, 2024).

4. "Disability Impacts All of Us," CDC Disability and Health Promotion, May 15, 2023, https://www.cdc.gov/ncbddd/disabilityandhealth/ infographic-disability-impacts-all.html; Yanmei Li, Qian Li, Juan Zheng, et al., "Prevalence and Trends in Diagnosed Learning Disability Among US Children and Adolescents from 1997 to 2021," *JAMA Pediatriatrics* 177, no. 9 (2023): 969–972, doi:10.1001/ jamapediatrics.2023.2117.

5. Ludmila N. Praslova, "How to Weigh the Risks of Disclosing a Disability," hbr.org, May 07, 2024, https://hbr.org/2024/05/ how-to-weigh-the-risks-of-disclosing-a-disability.

6. Doron Dorfman, "Fear of the Disability Con: Perceptions of Fraud and Special Rights Discourse," *Law & Society Review* 53, no. 4 (2019): 1051–1091, http://www.jstor.org/stable/45284585.

7. Iris Bohnet, "How to Take the Bias out of Interviews," hbr.org, April 18, 2016, https://hbr.org/2016/04/how-to-take-the-bias-out-of -interviews.

CHAPTER 13

How to Answer an Open-Ended Question from a Candidate

by Marlo Lyons

While interviewers often assume they hold all the power during the interview process, candidates are increasingly asking more insightful questions to assess whether they should make a move to a new company. Just as candidates prepare for interviews, interviewers need to put some thought into likely topics of conversation to be ready to answer open-ended questions

Adapted from "How to Answer an Open-Ended Question from a Job Candidate" on hbr.org, April 26, 2024 (product #H086YM).

from candidates—because your responses could either ignite their enthusiasm or dampen their interest in the opportunity.

Here are five strategies you can use to prepare for and address open-ended questions from candidates, with the goal of enticing them to eagerly pursue an open position with your company.

Know what information is confidential

Interviewers play a critical role in preserving confidentiality during the interview process, recognizing the sensitive nature of certain information that cannot be disclosed to candidates, even if they've signed a nondisclosure agreement (NDA). Understanding the boundaries of confidentiality is essential, as it protects proprietary information, trade secrets, and other sensitive data integral to the company's operations.

While NDAs offer legal protection, it's imperative for interviewers to exercise discretion and refrain from sharing confidential details such as upcoming product launches, strategic plans, or proprietary technologies during interviews. However, withholding information or stumbling while answering a question may project a lack of transparency within the company, which could turn off a candidate from wanting to work there. If you're unsure what information is confidential, discuss in advance with your manager or the legal department so you can confidently speak about confidential matters in a way that safeguards the company's interests while conveying enough information to satisfy the candidate.

If you're unable to share information, simply say, "I am so glad you asked that question. It gives me an understanding of how you think about the company. Unfortunately, I can't answer it because [e.g., of regulatory matters; of SEC disclosures; it's not public yet; I don't know the answer, but I will follow up with you]." Acknowledging the question will prevent a candidate from feeling like you're brushing them off or evading the question.

Prepare for common questions

Candidates often ask about company culture; for example, "Can you tell me about the culture?" or "What about the culture drew you to the company?" or "How has the culture changed over the last five years?" Instead of simply stating a preference for the culture or highlighting collaborative dynamics, it's essential to offer tangible examples or scenarios. The aim is to answer the question in a way that will give the candidate a good sense of how their working style would fit in and help them feel at ease about the prospect of joining the team, fostering a sense of comfort and belonging.

For example, you could talk about that time your cross-functional colleagues rallied to support you during a challenging project, displaying the organization's collaborative spirit. Or you could share a personal experience that illustrates the company's encouragement of work-life balance, such as how you're able to pick up your children every day at 3 p.m. or how you approach unplugging during vacations (and how you empower team members to do the same). And despite the passage of time since the Covid-19 lockdown, it's still valuable to describe how the company supported employees during that period, shedding light on its commitment to employee well-being and resilience.

The best reply to a question about culture always includes an example and the impact. For instance, "When we say our culture is built around 'One Team,' we mean it. That's what helps us maintain trust and ensure collaboration above personal interest. Just last week, our team was struggling to complete a major project. We alerted the broader team including cross-functional stakeholders. Everyone came together—including team members from other departments—to ensure we met our goal. Our goal is their goal. Their goal is our goal. That is how we view our work."

Another common question is about how the position came to be available. For example, "What is the history of this position?" or "What happened to the last person in this position?" The candidate is asking about whether the role is newly created or is vacant due to a departure or internal transfer. Transparency regarding the position's background, including its origins and any notable achievements or areas for improvement due to shifting needs, can give candidates valuable insight into role expectations. Additionally, discussing how the company decided to create a new role, the significance of the position, and how the person in the position will interact cross-functionally can help candidates better understand how their past experiences align with the job requirements.

Your answer should be short, clear, and if possible, related to the candidate. "This is a new position that we realized we needed to accelerate the business. Your skill set is exactly what we need." Or "This is a replacement position. The last person was promoted into a new role and is still at the company so he would be available for questions and onboarding to ensure your success." If the last person to hold the position left the company or was fired, consider saying something along the lines of "The last person held the position for three years and decided to depart the company for a new opportunity. We revised the position based on the current team needs. That's why I'm talking to you, because your skill set is right on point."

Connect answers to each candidate's skills and experience

Just as candidates strive to establish a connection during interviews, interviewers must do the same. When candidates ask questions about the position, relate your responses directly to their experience, citing specific examples from their résumé or interview answers.

For example, if the candidate asks how you'll measure success, draw parallels between their past achievements and the role's requirements. Maybe they previously gave you an example of how they created and led a specific marketing campaign targeting a diverse audience; you could answer their question by connecting their example to a role requirement of growing your product's reach to specific demographics and the corresponding key performance indicators for success.

For example, a candidate may ask, "What is the intangible thing you're looking for that's not on the job description?" Tailor your answer to align with information the candidate has already mentioned, such as "One of the main intangibles is someone who has innovated from white space, such as the creator of the first cell phone or digital watch. The story you told about how you were the innovator behind [unique technology] and how you used data to align the senior leadership toward pursuing it, is exactly the kind of visionary leadership we are looking for in this role."

Tying your answers directly to the candidate's skills and experience not only strengthens your connection, it also fosters a more meaningful and productive interview experience for each of you.

Highlight growth opportunities

As interviewers evaluate a candidate's potential fit within the company and team, candidates likewise assess whether their skills will be valued, if growth opportunities exist, and how their past experiences align with the company's goals.

Listen attentively during the interview to discern each candidate's short- and long-term aspirations. This will help you determine which company programs to highlight, from personalized coaching to educational courses to industry conferences. Discuss success stories of employees who have capitalized on the company's resources and growth opportunities, resulting in promotions or transitions to new roles that allow them to utilize their newly acquired skills. Be prepared to talk about how experience gained in the role could lead to particular career trajectories, as well as mentorship initiatives, training programs, and prospective projects that could help the candidate attain their career goals within the company, even if it means transitioning to a different department in the future.

For example, you could say something along the lines of "One of my risk analyst employees took advantage of our tuition reimbursement program to complete an MBA with a concentration in data science. I helped her find a mentor with one of our senior data scientists, which led to a stretch assignment with our data science team. The skills she acquired and the networking she did while working on that assignment positioned her to secure the next open data science position with the team. While it was sad to see her move onto a new team, I am proud of how hard she worked to reach her goals and I know she will bring even more value to the company. This is the kind of growth we actively support and encourage here, because we want high performers to know that they have a pathway for career advancement that is tailored to their individual aspirations."

Demonstrate self-awareness

Just as interviewers aim to select a candidate who will thrive within the company, candidates want assurance that they'll enjoy working for the hiring manager if they get the job. Candidates who are trying to understand whether the manager's leadership style will work for them may ask questions such as, "Can you tell me about a time when you feel like you failed an employee?"

or "How do you view your job in support of this role?" or "What is one quality in your leadership style that you expect your leaders to emulate?" You can seize the opportunity presented by these open-ended questions to candidly discuss your past mistakes, areas for improvement, and leadership approach, displaying vulnerability and fostering a sense of psychological safety for the candidate.

For example, you could demonstrate self-awareness in your response by saying something such as "I once failed an employee when I didn't provide enough guidance on a major project. I assumed they had everything under control and I didn't want to micromanage them, so I didn't dive into the details, and they missed a key deadline. Since then, I've made it a priority to have regular check-ins on major projects to ensure that my team feels comfortable asking for help or telling me when they're overwhelmed. I view my job as providing the resources and support my team needs to succeed. I expect my leaders to foster an environment where open communication and continuous improvement are encouraged. I learned a lot from this experience, specifically how to stay engaged and accessible while also empowering my team to own their work."

Interviewers should prepare for interviews just as thoroughly as candidates do. Being equipped with compelling stories and setting aside dedicated preparation time (for example, 30 minutes beforehand) allows interviewers to mentally prepare and be fully present during the interview. As with candidates, it's not only the content of what is said that matters, but also the manner in which it's conveyed. Demonstrating enthusiasm for the company and the position can leave a lasting impression on candidates, instilling confidence and enthusiasm in their decision-making process.

Marlo Lyons is a career, executive, and team coach, as well as the award-winning author of *Wanted—A New Career: The Definitive Playbook for Transitioning to a New Career or Finding Your Dream Job*. You can reach her at marlolyonscoaching.com.

CHAPTER 14

Should You Use AI to Assess Candidates?

by Tomas Chamorro-Premuzic and Reece Akhtar

Few things seem creepier than algorithms mining our voices, résumés, or photos to determine whether we should be considered for a job, and yet this is now the reality for most job seekers.[1] What's more, it may not be as creepy as you think.

For starters, all organizations struggle with talent identification, which is why many complain that they are unable to find the right person for key positions and

---

Adapted from "Should Companies Use AI to Assess Job Candidates?" on hbr.org, May 17, 2019 (product #H04YFM).

why most people end up in jobs that are far from inspiring.[2] Consider that even in the biggest economy in the world, where talent management practices are far more science-driven and sophisticated than anywhere else, the labor market is quite inefficient.

Today in the United States, there are around six million job seekers for eight million job openings.[3] Even if we look at the global knowledge economy, comprised of the most qualified and skilled cognitive elite (roughly the one billion people who are on LinkedIn), job satisfaction is the exception rather than the norm: It is estimated that as many as 70% of these top talented individuals are open to other, hopefully more meaningful or interesting, jobs or careers.[4] Elsewhere, the norm characterizing recruitment and hiring processes is considerably more backward, with hiring managers overemphasizing hard skills at the expense of the more important and critical soft skills or using intuitive yet biased hiring methods, such as the unstructured job interview, to determine who gets the job.[5] All the while, predictive assessments and data-driven tools are largely underutilized, and the prevalence of prejudice, bias, and discrimination is everywhere.[6]

In short, if we want to make talent identification more effective—and more meritocratic—it's important to continue to look beyond existing methods, particularly if recent technological innovations such as advances in machine-learning and generative artificial intelligence enable us to predict, understand, and match people at scale.

One of the major problems with the way we currently interview job candidates is that the process is largely unstructured, leaving the questioning to the whims and fancies of the interviewer. It shouldn't take much convincing to see how this is not only inefficient, but also leads to biased decision-making as interviewers express and seek to confirm their own preferences.[7]

Video or digital interviews can remove these limitations almost entirely. Using generative AI to create a highly structured and standardized interview experience, every candidate can be presented with the same set questions and be given the same opportunity to express their talent, which ultimately improves the video's predictive utility.[8]

But while digital interviews provide a fairer interview experience for candidates and allow organizations to access more diverse talent, when it comes to reviewing these interviews, we run into the same problems—biased humans are left to make the hiring decisions. But what if AI and machine-learning algorithms were tasked with mining the data from these videos to identify reliable connections between what people do and say during interviews, and their personality, ability, or job performance? In the case of digital interviews, AI algorithms can mine a candidate's facial expressions and body language, along with what they say and how they say it.[9]

Mining all this data can reveal a lot about the candidate's talent and can indicate how they might perform on the job. Scientific research in this area has been steadily growing, revealing interesting and promising findings.[10] For instance, researchers have trained algorithms that mine various characteristics of an individual's voice (e.g., vocal pitch, loudness, and intensity); body movement (e.g., hand gestures, posture, etc.); or facial expressions (e.g., happiness, surprise, anger) to accurately predict their personality profile, which we know is one of the leading predictors of job performance.[11]

Going further, researchers have mined similar signals to predict behaviors and qualities that are critical for performance: communication skills, persuasiveness, stress tolerance, and leadership.[12] Further revealing how insightful this technology truly is, a team of researchers used the aforementioned technologies to quantify the emotionality of CEOs as they spoke in conference calls to accurately predict the firm's future financial performance.[13]

AI has the potential to significantly improve the way we identify talent because it can reduce the cost of making accurate predictions about a candidate's potential while at the same time removing the bias and heuristics that so often cloud human judgment. The fact that AI algorithms can detect and measure latent or seemingly intangible human qualities may lead some to be skeptical of the findings discussed here, but it is worth noting that there are plenty of scientific studies that demonstrate that humans can accurately identify personality and intellect from just thin slices of verbal and nonverbal behavior.[14] AI algorithms simply leverage the same cues. The difference between humans and AI is that the latter can scale and can be automated. What's more, AI does not have an ego that needs to be managed.

Currently, many organizations that use digital interviews do not leverage these types of powerful AI analytics, as their recruiters are often unwilling to accept the algorithm's recommendations and continue to rely on their own naive judgement. Sadly, this behavior is harming both the candidate and the organization. The HR departments that realize that science and data, and not intuition or instinct, should be the basis for decisions will attract and retain the best talent. Of course, we do not advocate that all hiring decisions be made by an AI system. There must always be human oversight. Instead, we believe that human decisions can be significantly improved if there is accurate and valid data to inform and shape our judgments. For example, AI-enabled digital interviews can be used to analyze candidates' soft skills, technical competence, facial expressions, vocal tones, and body language. These insights can then be integrated into a comprehensive candidate profile, offering hiring managers a detailed and objective evaluation. This approach not only enhances the predictive validity of the hiring process but also reduces biases, leading to more equitable and effective hiring decisions. Importantly, it's also crucial to design these AI tools with user experience in mind to ensure a fair and transparent process that respects and engages candidates.

Of course, it's essential to consider the legal and ethical implications of using these innovative tech tools, just as we do when we consider using traditional assessment methods.[15] AI systems can end up learning all sorts of harmful biases of their own, depending on the data they're trained on, among other factors. There are new regulations from New York, California, and the European Union placing pressure on companies to pay attention to how these systems are trained, and also regularly audit them for potential bias.[16] Also, clearly, there is now a difference between what we *can* know about people, and what we *should* know about them, with the possibilities surpassing both legal and ethical boundaries.

Yet at the same time, it's still possible to deploy innovations like the ones we describe here while operating within the constraints of good codes of conduct. Candidates can be fully briefed and debriefed about the technologies being used to evaluate them, and should be invited to actively opt in. Organizations should fully protect and keep safe all sensitive data, and the entire process should be transparent. In fact, it is even possible (and advisable) for candidates to have ownership of their data and results, which they may voluntarily decide to share with selected recruiters and employers—or not. While this scenario may seem more utopian than the emerging technologies we described, we would like to urge recruiters and employers to consider it. After all, there is no tension between understanding job candidates well and helping them understand themselves better. Organizations—and individuals—will benefit enormously when new technologies can boost their ability to place the right person in the right job.

THREE STRATEGIES TO MATCH THE RIGHT TOOLS TO THE RIGHT PROCESSES

Making great hiring decisions is the result of matching the right tools with the right processes. Practice these three strategies to increase your chances of finding and recruiting the very best talent:

1. **Adopt structured and standardized practices:** To ensure a fair and consistent hiring process, organizations should adopt structured and standardized evaluation methods. By using a set of predetermined questions and criteria for all candidates, and implementing hiring scorecards, recruiters and hiring managers can objectively assess responses, minimizing the influence of personal biases. Structured interviews not only enhance the reliability of the hiring process but also provide a clear framework for comparing candidates on an equal footing.

2. **Leverage predictive assessments and analytics:** Incorporating scientifically-validated assessments and AI-driven tools can significantly enhance the accuracy of hiring decisions. Predictive assessments, such as cognitive ability tests and personality assessments, offer valuable insights into a candidate's potential beyond their résumé. AI and data analytics can further refine this process by analyzing video interviews for non-verbal cues, providing objective insights into a candidate's soft skills. These technologies help in identifying patterns and predicting success, thereby making the hiring process

(continued)

THREE STRATEGIES TO MATCH THE RIGHT TOOLS TO THE RIGHT PROCESSES

more data-driven and less reliant on subjective judgment.

3. **Focus on continuous training to mitigate bias:** Continuous training is crucial to keep hiring managers updated on the latest recruitment technologies and best practices. Regular workshops, webinars, and industry conferences can provide the necessary skills to use new tools effectively. Moreover, it's essential to provide bias training and conduct regular audits of hiring practices. This ensures that both human and AI decision-makers are free from prejudices, promoting a more inclusive and equitable hiring process. Ensuring that AI tools are trained on diverse datasets and regularly audited for potential biases is also critical.

Tomas Chamorro-Premuzic is the chief innovation officer at ManpowerGroup, a professor of business psychology at University College London and at Columbia University, cofounder of deepersignals.com, and an associate at Harvard's Entrepreneurial Finance Lab. He is the author of *Why Do So Many Incompetent Men Become Leaders? (and How to Fix It)*, upon which his TEDx Talk was based. His latest book is *I, Human: AI, Automation, and* *the Quest to Reclaim What Makes Us Unique.* Find him at www.drtomas.com.

Reece Akhtar is CEO and cofounder of Deeper Signals. He is an organizational psychologist, data scientist, and visiting lecturer at NYU. He is the author of *The Future of Recruitment: Using the New Science of Talent Analytics to Get Your Hiring Right.*

NOTES

1. Josh Bersin and Tomas Chamorro-Premuzic, "New Ways to Gauge Talent and Potential," *MIT Sloan Management Review*, November 16, 2018, https://sloanreview.mit.edu/article/new-ways-to-gauge-talent-and-potential/; T.T. Tran, T.G. Nguyen, T.H. Dang, and Y. Yoshinga, "Improving Human Resources' Efficiency with a Generative AI-Based Résumé Analysis Solution," in *Future Data and Security Engineering. Big Data, Security and Privacy, Smart City and Inudstry 4.0 Applications,* eds. T.K. Dang, J. Küng, T.M. Chung (FDSE), in *Communications in Computer and Information Science,* vol 1925 (Springer, Singapore 2023). https://doi.org/10.1007/978-981-99-8296-7_25; Sam Levin, "Face-Reading AI Will Be Able to Detect Your Politics and IQ, Professor Says," *The Guardian*, September 12, 2017, https://www.theguardian.com/technology/2017/sep/12/artificial-intelligence-face-recognition-michal-kosinski.

2. Jim Harter, "Dismal Employee Engagement Is a Sign of Global Mismanagement," Gallup, https://www.gallup.com/workplace/231668/dismal-employee-engagement-sign-global-mismanagement.aspx.

3. Stephanie Ferguson, "Understanding America's Labor Shortage," U.S. Chamber of Commerce, July 24, 2024, https://www.uschamber.com/workforce/understanding-americas-labor-shortage.

4. LinkedIn, "About LinkedIn," https://about.linkedin.com/; "The Ultimate List of Hiring Statistics," LinkedIn, https://business.linkedin.com/content/dam/business/talent-solutions/global/en_us/c/pdfs/Ultimate-List-of-Hiring-Stats-v02.04.pdf.

5. Saul Mcleod, PhD, "The Interview Method in Psychology," *Simply Psychology*, January 6, 2024, https://www.simplypsychology.org/interviews.html.

6. Tomas Chamorro-Premuzic, Dave Winsborough, Ryne A. Sherman, and Robert Hogan, "New Talent Signals: Shiny New Objects or a Brave New World?" *Industrial and Organizational Psychology: Perspectives on Science and Practice* 9, no. 3 (2016): 621–640, https://doi.org/10.1017/iop.2016.6.

7. Julie M. McCarthy, Chad H. Van Iddekinge, and Michael A. Campion, "Are Highly Structured Job Interviews Resistant to Demographic Similarity Effects?," *Personnel Psychology* 63 (2010): 325–359, https://doi.org/10.1111/j.1744-6570.2010.01172.x.

8. Willi H. Wiesner and Steven F. Cronshaw, "A Meta-Analytic Investigation of the Impact of Interview Format and Degree of Structure on the Validity of the Employment Interview," *Journal of Occupational Psychology* 61 (1988): 275-290, https://doi.org/10.1111/j.2044-8325.1988.tb00467.x.

9. Tomas Chamorro-Premuzic, Reece Akhtar, David Winsborough, and Ryne A. Sherman, "The Datafication of Talent: How Technology Is Advancing the Science of Human Potential at Work," *Current Opinion in Behavioral Sciences* 18 (2017): 13–16, DOI:10.1016/j.cobeha.2017.04.007.

10. L. Hickman, et al., "Automated Video Interview Personality Assessments: Reliability, validity, and generalizability investigations," *Journal of Applied Psychology*, August 2022;107(8):1323-1351. doi: 10.1037/apl0000695. Epub 2021 Jun 10. PMID: 34110849.

11. G. Mohammadi and A. Vinciarelli, "Automatic Personality Perception: Prediction of Trait Attribution Based on Prosodic Features," *IEEE Transactions on Affective Computing*, vol 3, no. 3, 273-284 (July-September 2012) doi: 10.1109/T-AFFC.2012.5; Ligia Batrinca, Nadia Mana, and Bruno Lepri et al., "Please, Tell Me About Yourself: Automatic Personality Assessment Using Short Self-Presentations," Proceedings of the 13th International Conference on Multimodal Interfaces, ICMI 2011, Alicante, Spain, November 14–18, 2011, 255–262, doi: 10.1145/2070481.2070528; Joan-Isaac Biel, Lucía Teijeiro-Mosquera, and Daniel Gatica-Perez, "FaceTube: Predicting Personality from Facial Expressions of Emotion in Online Conversational Video," Proceedings of the 14th ACM International Conference on Multimodal Interaction, ICMI 2012, 53–56, https://doi.org/10.1145/2388676.2388689; M. R. Barrick and M. K. Mount, "The Big Five Personality Dimensions and Job Performance: A Meta-Analysis," *Personnel Psychology*, 44 (1991): 1-26. https://doi.org/10.1111/j.1744-6570.1991.tb00688.x

12. Laurent Nguyen, Denise Frauendorfer, Marianne Mast, and Daniel Gatica-Perez, "Hire Me: Computational Inference of Hirability in Employment Interviews Based on Nonverbal Behavior," *IEEE Transactions on Multimedia* 16, no 4 (2014): 1018–1031, doi:10.1109/TMM.2014.2307169; Dairazalia Sanchez-Cortes, Oya Aran, Marianne S. Mast, and Daniel Gatica-Perez, "A Nonverbal Behavior Approach to Identify Emergent Leaders in Small Groups," *IEEE Transactions on Multimedia* 14, no. 3 (2012): 816–832, doi: 10.1109/TMM.2011.2181941.

13. William J. Mayew and Mohan Venkatachalam, "The Power of Voice: Managerial Affective States and Future Firm Performance," *Journal of Finance* 67 (2012): 1-43, https://doi.org/10.1111/j.1540-6261.2011.01705.x.

14. Peter Borkenau, Nadine Mauer, Rainer Riemann et al., "Thin Slices of Behavior as Cues of Personality and Intelligence," *Journal of Personality and Social Psychology* 86, no. 4 (2004): 599–614; Murphy, N. A., Hall, J. A., Schmid Mast, M., Ruben, M. A., Frauendorfer, D., Blanch-Hartigan, D., Roter, D. L., and Nguyen, L. (2015), "Reliability and Validity of Nonverbal Thin Slices in Social Interactions," *Personality and Social Psychology Bulletin*, 41(2), 199-213, https://doi.org/ 10.1177/0146167214559902.

15. National Research Council, "Ethical Issues Related to Personnel Assessment and Selection," in *New Directions in Assessing Performance Potential of Individuals and Groups: Workshop Summary* (Washington, DC: National Academies Press, 2013), https://doi .org/10.17226/18427.

16. Jonathan Kestenbaum, "NYC's New AI Bias Law Broadly Impacts Hiring and Requires Audits," Bloomberg Law, July 5, 2023, https://news.bloomberglaw.com/us-law-week/nycs-new-ai-bias-law -broadly-impacts-hiring-and-requires-audits; Benjamin M. Ebbink, Usama Kahf, Kile E. Marks, and Annie Ziesing, "A Glance at Proposed AI Bills in California," SHRM, April 5, 2024, https://www.shrm.org/ topics-tools/employment-law-compliance/a-glance-at-proposed-ai -bills-in-california; Patrick DiDomenico, "What Recent Global Regulations of AI Will Mean for HR," SHRM, April 8, 2024, https://www.shrm.org/topics-tools/employment-law-compliance/ what-recent-global-regulations-of-ai-will-mean-for-hr.

Ask Better Questions

CHAPTER 15

Seven Rules for Interview Questions That Result in Great Hires

by John Sullivan

Some of the long-held ideas about how to conduct interviews are no longer accurate. For example, there's no longer such thing as a surprise interview question. Candidates can prepare and video their practice interviews to the point where their responses are universally impressive, if not genuine or accurate.

Adapted from "7 Rules for Job Interview Questions That Result in Great Hires" on hbr.org, February 10, 2016 (product #H02NS8).

It's not just surprise questions that are a thing of the past. Research at firms like Google has proven that "brainteaser questions" can contribute to a costly mis-hire, that having a candidate meet any more than four interviewers doesn't increase new-hire quality, and that for many jobs, factors like grades, test scores, and schools attended don't predict success in the position.

It's time to rethink your interview questions with a focus on work-related questions that are harder to fake an answer to.

Avoid easy-to-practice questions

If you work for a major corporation, most of the interview questions used by hiring managers at your firm are publicly posted on Glassdoor.com—along with recommended answers. So start with a clean slate of questions, and at the very least eliminate overused and easy-to-practice questions with a low predictive value, like "What are your greatest strengths and weaknesses?" and "Why are you the best candidate?" and "What's your dream job?" and "Where would you like to be in five years?"

Be wary of historical questions

Questions that require a candidate to describe how they performed in the past, also known as "behavioral interview questions" (e.g., "Tell me about a time when you led . . . "), are problematic in a fast-moving world where yesterday's approaches quickly become irrelevant. And according to research by professors Frank Schmidt and John Hunter, those questions predict success only 12% better than a coin flip.[1] Why? Because the way a candidate did something years ago at another firm may be the wrong answer today at this firm with its unique culture. Historical questions also allow a good storyteller to passionately describe how a problem was solved even though they only played a minor role in the solution.

Assess their ability to solve a problem

If you were hiring a chef, you would ask them to cook a meal. Taking a "job content" approach by having an applicant do some of the actual work is the best way to separate top candidates from average ones. Consider asking them to:

- **Identify problems on the job.** Say something like: "Please walk me through the steps of the process that you'll use during your first weeks to identify the most important current problems or opportunities in your area."

- **Solve a current problem.** The ability to solve current problems is often the number one predictive factor of job performance. Provide them with a description of an actual problem that they'll face on their first day. Then ask them to walk you through the broad steps they would take to solve it. Prior to the interview, make a list of the essential steps. Deduct points if they omit important steps like gathering data, consulting with the team or customer, and identifying success metrics.

- **Identify the problems in your process.** Hand them a brief description of a flawed existing process related to their job. Ask them to examine the process and identify the top three areas where they predict serious problems are likely to occur. Prior to the interview, make a list of those pain points and flaws.

Evaluate whether they're forward-looking

In fast-evolving environments, employees must anticipate the future. Consider asking these questions to assess how well a candidate can do that:

- **Outline your plan for this job.** The very best employees develop a plan before they begin a major project or new job. Ask them to outline the elements of their plan of action for their first three to six months. Have them highlight key components, including goals, whom they'll consult with (by title), what data they'll analyze, how they'll communicate with their team, the metrics for assessing their plan's success, etc.

- **Forecast the evolution of the job/industry.** Anticipating major shifts is critical. Ask them to forecast at least five ways that their job will likely evolve over the next three years as a result of changes in the business environment. New hires must also be able to anticipate changes in your industry. So consider asking candidates to project three to five major trends in your industry and then forecast how the top firms will need to change over the next few years to meet those trends.

Assess a candidate's ability to learn, adapt, and innovate

If the job requires any of those factors, consider these questions:

- **Learning.** "Outline the steps you'd take to continuously learn and maintain your expert status in one important technical area."

- **Agility.** "Outline the steps you'd take to adapt when a dramatic unexpected change occurs in either technology or customer expectations."

- **Innovation.** "Outline the steps you'd take to increase innovation among your team to respond to increased competition or new technologies."

Allocate time for selling

The bulk of the interview time should be allocated to assessing the candidate, but set aside time to excite and sell candidates on the job and your firm. Proactively ask, "What are the top factors that you'll use to assess a job offer?" Then be sure to provide compelling information covering each "job acceptance factor."

Interviews are tough to get right. But research has shown that carefully selecting questions and determining acceptable answers ahead of time will increase your chances of success.[2] Research also shows that most hiring decisions are made within 15 seconds, so you must consciously avoid any judgments until the interview is at least 50% completed.[3]

—————————

John Sullivan, is a professor of management at San Francisco State University and an internationally known HR thought leader from the Silicon Valley. He's a prolific author, with over 900 articles and 10 books covering all areas of talent management.

NOTES

1. Frank Schmidt and John Hunter, "The Validity and Utility of Selection Methods in Personnel Psychology," *Psychological Bulletin* 124 (September 1998):262–274, doi: 10.1037/0033-2909.124.2.262.

2. Lou Adler, "Esteemed Harvard Professor Blasts Current Hiring Practices," LinkedIn, January 27, 2016, https://www.linkedin.com/pulse/esteemed-harvard-professor-blasts-current-hiring-practices-lou-adler/.

3. Malcolm Gladwell, "The New-Boy Network," *The New Yorker*, May 21, 2000, https://www.newyorker.com/magazine/2000/05/29/the-new-boy-network.

CHAPTER 16

Stop Asking Candidates the Wrong Questions

by Nilofer Merchant

I could tell right away from the tone of his voice that the VP of engineering wasn't happy. He practically growled at me. He had just finished interviewing a job candidate named Anand, who I had directed his way, and was calling me to say he was going to pass.

Just a few minutes earlier, Anand had called and raved about how well the interview had gone. He had interviewed for nearly a full day, meeting with different leaders across the organization, including, at the end of

---

Adapted from "Stop Eliminating Perfectly Good Candidates by Asking Them the Wrong Questions" on hbr.org, March 22, 2019 (product #H04UHV).

the day, the VP of engineering. I had helped this company build out a new "platform" strategy, which is why I was trying to identify the right candidates to work on it, and I thought Anand would be a great fit.

But the VP and Anand had strikingly different reports about their meeting. Anand said that he had asked far more questions than he usually did, asking for detailed and specific information on the strategy that helped him understand the complexity of the challenges the company was facing. He felt like he had held engaging, insightful conversations with everyone he met. In contrast, the VP told me that he found Anand's questions "super annoying."

This isn't the first time I've heard a leader say that a perfectly qualified candidate is a "bad fit." Candidates are too often screened out because they don't fit a particular pattern—one survey found as many as 75% of résumés don't make it past applicant tracking systems.[1] As I discussed the issue further with the VP, I learned that he thought that Anand had the right skills and experience but that he found Anand's questions annoying. He said: "He asked us a ton of questions that the team didn't have the answers to." His assessment that Anand was a "bad fit" was really code for "I don't want to feel uncomfortable."

Innovation requires not knowing long enough to learn new things. How can you build something new if you aren't okay with not already knowing the answer? The future is not created; it's co-created. Leaders need to build teams that can both *define* the right questions, and then *discover* new answers.

Instead of being annoyed by Anand's questions, the VP should've welcomed them—and asked Anand questions in turn. That is, of course, the value of an interview. An employer seeks to learn about the candidate's skills and relevant experiences. And a good candidate uses questions to learn about the role, the boss, and the company to assess whether it's the right job. Here are some types of questions the VP might've asked—and the ones you should ask—to avoid screening out a perfectly good candidate based on the wrong criteria.

Questions that uncover capabilities, not just experience

Are you asking questions that get to someone's *capabilities* or are you seeking confirming data that someone has done exactly what you have already scoped? Several years ago, a colleague asked if I'd review their job description for a social media "expert." Twitter had been around for maybe a year at this point and when I looked at the description, I just started laughing. The first line read "10 years of experience." Quite often, we use useless metrics to scope a job to do what has already been done. The upside of asking for years of experience is we get someone who has done what we need. The downside is we risk limiting what we can create next by doing what has already worked. Instead of asking, "Have you done x or y or z?" you want to ask, "How *would you approach* doing x or y or z?"

Unfortunately, an estimated 77% of all jobs (60% in the U.S. and 80% worldwide) require little to no creativity, decision-making, or independent judgment. But if you are working on innovation, you need someone who can *think with you*. And by focusing on capability over experience, you increase the chances you find that person.

Questions that assess whether they can co-create on a team

When I ask the teams I've worked with in the last 10 years why their last major strategic effort failed, they rarely mention that the team didn't get along. But they do say that there were cracks in the team—roles that weren't being filled—and that no one was able to step in to fill them. Because the world changes quickly, the work does too, and team members can't stay in their pre-determined roles. Teams need to figure out new terrain together. You might ask candidates, "How would you handle a situation where it's become clear that there is a gap on your team?" Interviewees are often told to use "I" to get credit for work done, but "we" is probably a more realistic depiction of how work gets done. Then follow up to learn how they felt about the situation: Were they proud of catching the gap? Concerned that it existed in the first place? This will help you see if you are dealing with a team player or a know-it-all. You want to find people who can play together, filling in the gaps between predefined roles to get the work done.

Questions that uncover the kinds of things they love to work on

If you're hiring for innovation, you need to ask what this person authentically brings to work. Ideas, after all, are not invented and grown in a vacuum; they grow and evolve by connecting previously separate elements. Figuring out what people genuinely care about lets you put people together who don't have the same approaches but who want to reach the same goal. It's that connection where innovation happens. But people need to be united around a shared purpose and focused on something that has meaning to them. Ask candidates, "What did you find meaningful about that project?" "What does that particular success say about what matters to you?" People want to match their purpose to the organizations they work for. And it's your job as the leader to align that purpose so that seemingly disparate people can come together into an "us" headed in the same direction.

Too often, leaders screen out perfectly good candidates because they don't understand how to hire people for co-creative problem-solving. It's easy to forget that the job of a leader isn't to know all the answers but to create the conditions by which the entire team gets to learn and innovate.

In the end, the VP did hire Anand—and together they've realized the goals they set out to achieve.

———————

Nilofer Merchant has personally launched 100 products amounting to $18 billion in revenue and has served on both public and private boards. Today, she lectures at Stanford, gives talks around the world, and has been ranked one of the most influential management thinkers in the world by Thinkers50. Her latest book is *The Power of Onlyness: Make Your Wild Ideas Mighty Enough to Dent the World.*

NOTE

1 Sanjoe Jose, "The Demise of Applicant Tracking Systems," Talview, January 21, 2016, https://blog.talview.com/en/demise-of -applicant-tracking-system.

CHAPTER 17

Five Qualities to Look for in a New Hire

by Shanna Hocking

A great leader knows that their team members play a significant role in their and the organization's success. That's why understanding how to make a strong hire is an important skill for new managers to learn. Though you'll have a limited time with each candidate during the interview process, you can maximize that time by asking strategic questions to gain insights into their strengths and weaknesses. Ultimately, this can help you make more thoughtful hiring decisions.

As a team leader, hiring manager, and now coach, I've reviewed hundreds of résumés and successfully

Adapted from content posted on hbr.org, March 4, 2024.

onboarded many employees who've gone on to thrive in their careers. Earlier on, I also made some hiring decisions that weren't right for either my teams or the candidates. Through all of this, I've learned a few valuable traits that new managers should consider when given the opportunity to make an addition to their teams.

Here are five traits to look for when interviewing for candidates who will benefit nearly every team, as well as the workplace culture.

Trait 1: Entrepreneurial Mindset

An entrepreneurial spirit isn't only for people who want to start their own business. Employees who demonstrate entrepreneurial qualities, such as being self-motivated and taking the initiative to create solutions to problems, can enhance any team. For example, an employee who sees challenges and believes they can solve them, or work through them, will help your organization achieve more than someone who gets easily frustrated by barriers. Plus, someone who naturally has, or who has done the work to develop, an entrepreneurial mindset is more likely to feel a sense of commitment and ownership to the organizational outcomes.[1]

Particularly if you're in an industry where people hear "no" often (something common for the fundraising work I do), look for these employees—many of whom will see rejection as learning opportunities or chances to find a better approach or solution. This mindset will help them navigate the complexity of the role.

Interview questions to measure this skill

- Tell me about a time you pursued a work project that others didn't believe would be possible (or that others said had been tried before and wouldn't work).

- How have you improved a process or project in an organization?

Clues to look for in their answers

An entrepreneurial spirit, or a drive to solve challenges, isn't necessarily something people know they have. But it is reflected in how they develop plans, the decisions they make in stressful situations, and their willingness to try something again that previously didn't go as planned. The candidate may give examples about navigating a complex work environment or convey a sense of pride in the projects they contribute to. Look for cues that a candidate thinks creatively, is open to sharing ideas, adapts to unforeseen circumstances, and shows resilience.

Trait 2: Curiosity

Curiosity can be a cornerstone of building a strong organizational culture. Employees who demonstrate curiosity ask questions to learn more about the world and the people around them. They show willingness to experiment with new ideas and they bring a learning mindset to the role and workplace. When employees feel they can challenge the status quo, it leads to more innovation and creativity.[2]

Curious employees want to learn the "why" that's driving the actions of their employer, team members, customers, and industry, which will help your organization adapt and evolve.

Interview questions to measure this skill

- Tell me about a time you pursued a learning opportunity on your own (without being assigned or asked by your manager).

- What do you most enjoy learning about?

Clues to look for in their answers

Listen for how a candidate shares excitement about what they've learned recently or what they want to learn more about in the future. They might reference something they read or listened to that sparked their interest.

A candidate's natural curiosity may also emerge when they follow up this answer to ask you about your own learning interests or how your organization supports learning, because they'll want to find a manager who shares this commitment. If a candidate asks many questions during the interview, it can feel overwhelming to a hiring manager. But remember, the candidate is interviewing you as much as you're interviewing them.

Trait 3: Leading from Where They Are

Employees often confuse title and authority with the ability to influence and lead. Everyone has the potential to serve as a leader if they approach leadership as the energy and purpose by which they lead themselves and serve others.

I often tell my clients that "leading from where they are" is one of the best ways to advance their careers and grow within an organization. Employees who find ways to work within organizational boundaries to create meaningful progress while leveraging their genuine relationships and expertise—even without being in a formal position of power—help to develop strong organizations.

Interview questions to measure this skill

- Tell me about a time you took initiative at work on something that benefited your whole team.

- Tell me about a time you influenced your colleagues to move something forward or try something new.

Clues to look for in their answers

Listen for how a candidate creates their own opportunities, raises their hand for projects, and supports their colleagues and the organizations' larger goals. For example, they may say they developed a new initiative, championed the adoption of a new process, or successfully led a committee of peers. A candidate who answers both the first and second question with clear examples demonstrates a pattern of leading from where they are.

Trait 4: Self-Awareness

Self-awareness at work looks like reflecting on your strengths, behaviors, and feelings to better understand how each area relates to your actions, your team, and your environment.

A self-aware employee proudly knows their strengths and what areas they need to develop further, which they actively work toward. This understanding of both their strengths and weaknesses contributes to a positive relationship with others. For example, when a team member feels confident in their own skills and abilities, and also respects their colleagues' strengths and perspectives, it can lead to better communication and collaboration—and ultimately a stronger team.

Interview questions to measure this skill

- What are your superpowers?

- What is a misperception people have about you at work?

- How would a colleague describe you?

Clues to look for in their answers

Most people believe they're self-aware, but they're likely not as aware as they think. Listen to how a candidate says a colleague would describe them, which reflects their understanding of their relationship to others.

A candidate who isn't highly self-aware might be confused by the suggestion that there are misconceptions about them in the workplace, for example. Remember that self-awareness is an ongoing process, so listen for the candidate to share what they're continuing to improve on to demonstrate their commitment to their personal growth.

Trait 5: Growth Potential

An employee with growth potential has ambition and drive, which benefits them and your organization. With ongoing support and resources, you can position the employee to strengthen your organization now and in the future. I'm not suggesting that you hire with the intention of retaining an employee forever, but do give thought to how a new hire will be able to grow within their role and your organization over time. Employees want to have a sense of what their future may look like in a new organization; as their boss, you should be committed to helping your team members reach their potential.

Ultimately, hiring for potential, rather than solely focusing on performance, can give you access to untapped talent and help you build a team of loyal employees who are grateful to work at a place that nurtures and invests in their professional development.

Interview questions to measure this skill

- How did you grow in your most recent role?

- What do you want to do differently/more of in your next role?

Clues to look for in their answers

A candidate with growth potential will provide examples of how they've improved themselves and their organization through their own initiative. They'll likely have clear ideas of what they'd like to learn or try in their new role in order to expand their experience and skill set. Review their résumé for additional insights. For example, an internal promotion recognizes that an employee continued to add value to an organization over time (as determined by people who evaluated their work outcomes).

Keep in mind, hiring isn't about finding the perfect person for the role. Perfect doesn't exist. Look for someone who has meaningfully contributed to other organizations and teams and who is excited to add value to your organization and team, too. Hiring well will become part of your legacy as a manager, and it's one of the ways you can directly and positively influence your organization's—and your new hire's—future.

————————

Shanna Hocking is the founder and CEO of Hocking Leadership, which specializes in leadership development and philanthropic strategy. Previously a senior executive at billion-dollar nonprofit organizations, she is a sought-after coach, consultant, and keynote speaker. She is also the author of *One Bold Move a Day: Meaningful Actions to Help Women Fulfill Their Leadership and Career Potential.*

IDENTIFY—AND HIRE—LIFELONG LEARNERS

by Marc Zao-Sanders

Talent management has undergone a massive overhaul, accelerated by the Covid-19 pandemic. Working environments, business priorities, and new technologies have been adopted with prodigious urgency. Hiring and onboarding have become substantially remote activities. In January 2020—even before Covid appeared—the World Economic Forum called for a global reskilling revolution, and firms now require different skills of their workforces, including resilience, adaptability, digital, design, and interpersonal capabilities.[a]

These changes have been a challenge for job candidates and employers alike. But I believe that there's a simple way to bring some much-needed clarity and guidance—one that adds value all the way along the employee life cycle, from hiring to managing performance.

The secret is to ask of people a simple question: *How do you learn?*

This is not about simplistic learning preferences (such as schedules and modalities) or broadly discredited learning styles (such as being a visual or aural learner).[b] This is about an individual's personal system for updating, improving, and sharing her knowledge and skills. Does the job candidate you're considering have such a system? And, for that matter, do you?

This may be the most pertinent question one can ask of a current or future employee. An individual's future performance is just as much a function of high-caliber, systematic, intentional skills development as it is of past achievements and qualifications, the traditional fare of job interviews.[c] And the capability and much of the value of a company is, in turn, a function of the collective skills of its workforce.

(continued)

IDENTIFY—AND HIRE—LIFELONG LEARNERS

Lifelong learning is now roundly considered to be an economic imperative and "the only sustainable competitive advantage."[d] Job candidates and employees who consider, update, and improve their skills are the high performers, especially over the longer term. Pressing ourselves on the question of how we learn brings a hard, pragmatic edge to the important but nebulous notion of growth mindset.

Let's consider the question's application to a key stage of the employee lifecycle: hiring.

Hiring and Getting Hired

Suppose the question were asked by default during the screening process. Convincing answers would indicate high levels of curiosity, organization, and method.

As a hiring manager:

- *Take care to be inclusive and open-minded about what counts as learning.* This is partly to be able to appreciate cultural and personal differences. It's also to recognize that there is a dizzying proliferation of content from which one can learn: courses, books, people, poems, performance support tools, songs, films, conversations, observations, reflections, memories, and more.[e] How does the candidate go about making sense of all of this? How do they face up to content overload? How do they select what's most relevant and then slice, dice, and digest it in a way that improves their feeling of fulfillment and level of performance over the long term?

- *Ask the candidate about something they've recently learned* and how they could apply it in the role for which you are considering them.

- *Be prepared to have the same question be asked of you.* Show an awareness of the skills deemed to be of particularly high value at the firm—this is typically a list of 20 to 100 skills, behaviors, and values, defined with care.

a. Saadia Zahidi, "We Need A Global Reskilling Revolution—Here's Why," World Economic Forum, January 22, 2020, https://www.weforum.org/agenda/2020/01/reskilling-revolution-jobs-future-skills/

b. Olga Khazan, "The Myth of 'Learning Styles,'" The Atlantic, April 11, 2018, https://www.theatlantic.com/science/archive/2018/04/the-myth-of-learning-styles/557687/.

c. Daniel Pacthod and Michael Park, "'Look for Skills, Not Credentials': Beth Cobert on Tapping Into US Talent," mckinsey.com, February 26, 2021, https://www.mckinsey.com/capabilities/people-and-organizational-performance/our-insights/look-for-skills-not-credentials-beth-cobert-on-tapping-into-us-talent?cid=other-eml-alt-mip-mck&hdpid=1662ed5f-e61e-4253-bd72-4451dbbcc783&hctky=9621023&hlkid=dc8941dda7d541509abeoc5f5d0d9998.

d. "Lifelong Learning Is Becoming an Economic Imperative," The Economist, January 12, 2017, https://www.economist.com/special-report/2017/01/12/lifelong-learning-is-becoming-an-economic-imperative; Arie de Geus, "Planning as Learning," Harvard Business Review, March 1988, https://hbr.org/1988/03/planning-as-learning.

e. Marc Zao-Sanders, "Filter!," Filtered blog, accessed August 26, 2024, https://learn.filtered.com/thoughts/filter.

(continued)

IDENTIFY—AND HIRE—LIFELONG LEARNERS

_____

Marc Zao-Sanders is CEO and cofounder of filtered.com, which develops algorithmic technology to make sense of corporate skills and learning content. He's the author of *Timeboxing: The Power of Doing One Thing at a Time.* Find Marc on LinkedIn or at www.marczaosanders.com.

Adapted from content posted on hbr.org, May 13, 2021 (product #H06CYJ).

NOTES

1. Jon L. Pierce, Tatiana Kostova, and Kurt T. Dirks, "Toward a Theory of Psychological Ownership in Organizations," *Academy of Management Review* 26, no. 2 (2001): 298–310, https://doi.org/10.2307/259124.

2. Siyuan Wang, "The Curvilinear Relationship Between Dissatisfaction with the Status Quo and Innovative Behavior," *Frontiers in Psychology* 13 (2022), doi.10.3389/fpsyg.2022.849586.

CHAPTER 18

Evaluate Responses to Common Interview Questions

by Xena Wang

You've received a great response to the job you've posted. You've worked with HR to narrow your list of potential candidates and schedule interviews. You've done all your prep work, and you have your list of questions prepared. How will you measure the responses the candidates provide? What does a "good" answer to some of the most common interview questions look like?

Adapted from "Good (and Bad) Answers to Common Interview Questions" on hbr.org, February 14, 2024.

Good vs. Bad Answers

As a first step, it's useful to understand what components differentiate a good and bad answer to common interview questions.

A good answer includes narratives or examples that are:

- Specific, clear, and self-aware

- Relatively recent

- Related to the core competencies highlighted in the job description

A bad answer includes narratives or examples that are:

- Too personal, unprofessional, or irrelevant

- Overly negative

- A poor reflection on your character or skills

With this information in mind, here are some things to look for in candidates' responses to some of the common questions you might pose.

Question #1: Why are you interested in this role?

Perhaps this role is the perfect next step in the candidate's career trajectory, or maybe it's a lateral move that has better benefits. It could be a back-up role the candidate applied to because the job market is competitive, or a stretch position they weren't expecting to be called in for. Whatever the circumstance, you'll want the candidate to focus their answer on two things:

- Specific aspects of the role that they find compelling and why. (How does the role align with their career goals?)

- The value they would bring to the team or organization through this role. (What can they offer you, given their unique skills and background experience?)

Scenario

A candidate works at a tech company as a programmer, but they want to pivot into a primarily client-facing role. The candidate already has a deep understanding of technological developments and coding. They want a job that combines their expertise and provides increased opportunities to engage with the software's users. To achieve this, they are interviewing for a sales associate position at a prominent software company.

> **Bad answer:** *I saw that the position was open, and I wanted to apply because I'm not fulfilled in my current job. I spend most of my time working on the computer, but I want to travel more and talk to people. Based on the job description, I think this role could be interesting since it involves more face-to-face interaction with clients.*

This is a bad response because it's vague. It focuses solely on what the candidate wants without explaining *why* interacting with customers is important to them or how it fits into their current career goals. It also fails to explain the value they would add as a new hire.

> **Good answer:** *I'm excited for this role because I've been looking to build more in-person client relationships. In my current role, I've developed strong technical skills, and I see this as an opportunity to use my expertise to help our customers better understand our products and choose the ones that best fit their needs.*
>
> *I see that this job requires 50% travel or more, which excites me as I'm someone who enjoys experiencing new environments and people, but also having a home base I can return to.*
>
> *Right now, I'm mostly working independently at my computer. I've still managed to cultivate strong relationships with various clients in the past couple of years, but I would thrive on the opportunity to travel and meet them face-to-face. Being in-person would also help me better understand their pain points and how to solve them. When it comes to problem solving, I think communication is much easier for both parties in-person than over a screen when possible.*

Unlike the bad response, the candidate in this example focuses on the positive aspects of their present role while also explaining the opportunities the new role would provide them. In addition, they explain how those opportunities better align with their current goals and how their contributions would benefit the company and its clientele.

Question #2: Tell me about a time when you worked well as part of a team

Here you're looking for the candidate to showcase transferable soft skills like collaboration, adaptability, and communication. These are key skills that would be beneficial in nearly all work environments and teams. This question can also be an opportunity for the candidate to showcase their leadership expertise.

Scenario

A college senior is preparing for their job search before graduation. They aren't sure what industry they want to pursue yet, but they know they enjoy—and are good at—leading teams. The senior is interviewing for an event planner role at a local nonprofit that hosts fundraisers and community programs.

> **Bad answer:** *Last semester, I had a group project for a history class presentation. I took the lead by telling everyone to take one part and to meet back again in two weeks. I did my work, my classmates did theirs, and we grouped it all together at the end. Our professor said we had a great presentation.*

This response at least underscores teamwork since the group accomplished their assignment. However, it lacks emphasis on three things: effective communication (ordering people to take part rather than discussing work division), collaboration (everyone only doing their part and bringing it together in the end), and specificity (role responsibilities and project road map).

Good answer: *Last semester, we had a four-person group project for our history class. My classmates were unsure who would tackle which part, so I took action and delegated the tasks: one each for research, outline, graphics, and speaking.*

Since public speaking is my strength, I offered to present on behalf of the group. The project was due in two weeks, so I scheduled a couple of midweek check-ins—both for accountability and to make sure that our content was on the right track.

There was an instance where a team member didn't get the outline by our check-in time, which delayed the graphics creation. I spoke with the individual to let them know that our grade relied on all of us working together and supporting each other. They understood where I was coming from and submitted their outline the next day.

Ultimately, we finished the project on time—and our professor said it was one of the best presentations in recent years!

This response shows how the candidate took initiative by discussing and assigning upcoming tasks. It also shows how the candidate worked well in a team setting: first, by noticing friction with a member neglecting their assignment; then, by speaking with the person and communicating the group's shared responsibilities in order to resolve the issue. As a bonus, it also reflects how the candidate's collaborative leadership led to a successful outcome.

Question #3: Have you ever had difficulty working with a manager or other team members?

When the candidate answers this question, you'll be listening to hear if they remain respectful and professional—even if they worked with a nightmare manager or on a dysfunctional teams. Everyone has disagreements at times—including the highest-performing teams—but that doesn't mean people can't work together toward a common goal.

Be wary of candidates who criticize, blame, or complain. You're looking for the candidate to stay neutral and stick to the facts.

Scenario

A midlevel employee is excited about a senior learning and development role at a rival pharmaceutical company. This new position encompasses designing and implementing programs from interns to the C-suite. On their own, the employee has already created sessions on onboarding, upskilling, and career growth. However, this senior L&D job requires collaborative input from multiple individuals across departments.

Bad answer: Yes. I had a disagreement with a colleague who wanted things done her way. Basically, I planned to run a career-building webinar for our summer interns. I took the initiative to reach out to one of our partners with HR expertise to participate, but this colleague was upset that I didn't consult her first since she's the liaison for this person.

I told her I was trying to streamline the requests so we could launch the webinar quickly. The colleague didn't see my perspective and thought I was upstaging her. She told me that moving forward, I'd have check in with her before contacting this HR partner.

Anyway, I've since organized nine professional development webinars. I've also come up with creative methods that don't involve waiting for their approval so we can launch these events faster.

While the candidate didn't explicitly belittle their colleague, their negative tone suggests that they think the colleague overreacted in the situation. Although this answer does highlight their accomplishments, it ultimately demonstrates how they don't take accountability or collaborate to find solutions.

Good answer: *I had a misunderstanding with a teammate regarding project communication. I wanted to ask one of our partners with HR expertise to participate in a career-building webinar for our summer interns. However, I overlooked informing my teammate, who was the liaison for this colleague, and she felt like I was trying to overshadow her role.*

Instead of letting this misinterpretation escalate, I initiated a private conversation with her to communicate my intentions. I apologized for not looping her in before contacting our HR partner and reassured her that moving forward, I would first check in with her about project tasks.

Together, we found a compromise that strengthened our working relationship and responsibilities. She's continued to be a great help in setting up similar professional development webinars.

A good response like this reflects the candidate's ability to handle challenging people and situations constructively. This answer also states the obstacles, the efforts made trying to resolve them, and the results.

Question #4: Tell me about a time you failed

This feels like a trick question—and to some extent, it is. You want the candidate to share an experience introducing a minor lapse in judgment and how they learned and improved from it. Red flags include an example that's too serious (such as a mistake that got the candidate fired) or that's related to your role's core competencies. The ideal answer will explain the situation, consequences, and solution.

Scenario

A consultant with two years of experience is grateful to have learned about various industries in their job. Now, they wish to focus solely on public policy analysis. Consulting has made them comfortable with high-pressure, fast-paced environments, and they are well prepared to transition into similar settings. Furthermore, the candidate also finds overlaps between this job opportunity and their consulting history: collaborating with several stakeholders to identify and solve problems—all while operating under strict timelines.

Bad answer: I didn't submit a report on time for a critical client presentation, which impacted the timeline and reflected poorly on our team. My manager was upset since she knows I'm not normally like that. I apologized to her, but we did end up losing the client.

This is a bad answer because while it addresses the failure, it doesn't acknowledge how the candidate learned from their mistake. It only touches on the issue and aftermath.

Good answer: During a particularly hectic work period, I didn't submit a report on time for a client presentation. This impacted the project timeline and our team's reputation. My manager was upset since this lapse was uncharacteristic of my usual behavior. I then took immediate responsibility by personally apologizing to my manager, my colleagues, and especially the clients.

The clients were understandably frustrated but appreciated my accountability. After that event, I implemented new strategies for myself to improve time management skills and communication with teammates when I needed support to meet deadlines. I also helped our team develop a contingency reference PDF that will help prevent similar situations in the future.

This response shows that we all make mistakes at work (they're inevitable), but what we do after messing up matters more. It shows how the candidate handled the mistake, which reveals their integrity and resilience in difficult circumstances. Those are the kind of people that make up strong teams.

Interviews are meaningful opportunities to explore a candidate's experience, mindset, and skills. As you consider how these qualities align with the role and your organization, listen with these pointers—and an open mind.

———————

Xena Wang (pronounced Zenna) is experienced in executive search, higher education, arts and culture, and nonprofits. She is an advocate for empowering individuals' personal and professional growth and fostering meaningful relationships across generations. A graduate of Swarthmore College and Harvard Extension School's Museum Studies program, Xena is involved in her community through the Swarthmore Alumni Council, Harvard Club of Philadelphia, and coleading the Philadelphia H4A chapter.

Assess Candidates and Make a Decision

CHAPTER 19

When to Take a Chance on a Candidate

by Rebecca Knight

Sometimes a job description and request for applications yields less-than-ideal candidates. How do you evaluate someone you know isn't exactly right for the position? How do you know which qualities are workable and which should be nonstarters? At what point should you take a leap of faith?

What the Experts Say

First things first: You're never going to find the perfect candidate for your job opening. "The perfect candidate

Adapted from "When to Take a Chance on an Imperfect Job Candidate" on hbr.org, March 8, 2021 (product #H0685J).

does not exist," says Claudio Fernández-Aráoz, a senior adviser at global executive search firm Egon Zehnder and the author of *It's Not the How or the What but the Who*. Besides, "even if the candidate does exist, it's [not a given that they would even] consider taking the job." In that sense, every applicant you're evaluating is inadequate in one way or another. "And they're not really flawed—they're just inferior to your dream candidate," says John Sullivan, professor of management at San Francisco State University and author of *1000 Ways to Recruit Top Talent*. Still, he says, all imperfect candidates are not created equal. "A bad hire can do a lot of damage."

Here are some tips on how to decide which job candidates you can work with even if they don't fulfill all the requirements.

Be data driven

When the HR department draws up the profile of the ideal candidate for your open req, the result is often "some combination of Superman, Batman, and Spider-Man," says Fernández-Aráoz. Since superheroes are in short supply in the labor market, Sullivan recommends being more objective and data driven in how you define what you seek in a candidate. "Look at the 10 people you have already doing the job. Then ask: What do the top three performers have in common? What characteristics do they share?" The answers will provide insight into the basic requirements of the role. "That's what's needed to succeed in the job, and you will assess candidates on those factors," says Sullivan.

If an applicant lacks one of the qualifications you've deemed necessary, it's an indication that they can't do the job. The objective of this exercise is to help you see more clearly which flaws are fatal and which are constructs designed by HR. For instance, you shouldn't automatically discount "someone who was a job hopper, or who was out of the workforce for two years, or who doesn't have a certain job title or degree," Sullivan says. "Some of the best web designers in the world don't have a degree in web design."

Assess capacity for learning

Even some serious inadequacies are surmountable, according to Fernández-Aráoz. "Hiring managers tend to weigh knowledge and skills, but that has many limitations," he says. Knowledge is easy to acquire and skills can be developed, so if an otherwise promising candidate lacks a particular skill, you don't need to write them off. "You want someone who has the capacity to continue to grow and learn," he says. The past is precedence, adds Sullivan. Because certain skills can be learned, find out whether anyone else at the organization has ever learned that specific skill on the job and done well. It's also worthwhile to ask candidates to describe the steps they take to learn something new. "Find out if they have a network to help them learn," says Sullivan. An inability to learn—or, worse, a lack of interest in doing so—are flaws too great to be conquered.

Measure potential

When the drawback in question is something like a nonstandard career trajectory, your appraisal should focus on whether the candidate has the "hallmarks and predictors of potential," says Fernández-Aráoz. These include attributes like curiosity, engagement, determination, confidence, and motivation. He recommends using structured interviews in which you ask each candidate the same set of defined questions. Of course, "you need to ask the right questions and draw the right inferences," he says, otherwise, you risk being fooled. "Even a psychopath can be highly engaging," he adds.

Say, for instance, you're trying to assess the applicant's strategic orientation. "You need to look at behavioral indicators that suggest this candidate is curious." Fernández-Aráoz suggests asking questions like, "Tell me about a situation in which you proactively sought feedback. What did you do with the results? And what were the consequences of that?" The quality of your candidate's response will indicate whether the flaw can be ameliorated.

Gather second (and third) opinions

And yet, don't take those responses as gospel. It's wise to scrutinize what your flawed applicant tells you, says Sullivan. "The world has changed," he says. "Because of Glassdoor, people already know the questions you're going to ask, and they know the answers, too." That's a boon to all applicants, but a challenge for hiring managers. Be rigorous—Sullivan recommends recording your interviews and rewatching them to validate your impressions. "Bring in outside managers for second opinions," he adds. Sullivan is also a proponent of peer interviews. Peers who will likely be working side by side with the candidate will be able to discern the severity of the weakness. "The best people to judge are those who are already doing the job. They're the ones who understand the job better than the manager, and they can predict success."

Provide multiple assessments

Of course, interviews by themselves are not enough to evaluate a typical job candidate—let alone one who's flawed. Sullivan recommends so-called "whiteboard tests" to determine whether or not their limitations would keep them from being able to do the job.

These tests, popular in Silicon Valley, aim to measure an engineer's problem-solving skills. Candidates are given a code problem or task and a whiteboard, and they must work out their code and communicate their solution. The aim is to "give candidates a real problem they would have to solve on their first day," says Sullivan. These tests are transferable to other industries and functions. Going in, you, the hiring manager, "know that certain parts of the solution are non-negotiable." For instance, adds Sullivan, if you ask prospective salespeople to write up their process and in doing so, they fail to ask their customers what they want, it's a sign that they can't work for you.

Gauge emotional intelligence

Your assessment should not involve a consideration of whether you "want to grab a beer with your candidate" or whether "they're nice and energetic," says Sullivan. Indeed, those are the sort of superficial "flaws" that are famous sources of bias in the hiring process. And yet, it's important to gauge your flawed candidate's interpersonal skills. "People are hired because of their academic achievement and experience, but they're fired for their emotional intelligence"—or lack thereof—says Fernández-Aráoz.

Every desirable job candidate exhibits a certain degree of self-awareness, but this trait is especially important for less-than-ideal candidates. They need to know what they don't know and have good relationship-management skills and social awareness to cultivate colleagues so they can learn what they need to, adds Fernández-Aráoz. He also recommends reference checks to help you better understand the candidate. Talking to your candidate's former managers and colleagues will help you ascertain whether this person has the people skills or adaptability to thrive at your organization.

Don't compromise on character

It's also important to assess whether what you perceive as a weakness or personality flaw is, in fact, a relevant issue in terms of the role you have open, according to Fernández-Aráoz. In a lot of jobs, for instance, you think you want a candidate who exhibits optimism—"that's particularly true of sales jobs." However, if the role you're looking to fill is for a controller, optimism would be a problem. "In this case, you want a pessimistic soul who spends sleepless nights ruminating" on all the things that could go wrong.

There is, however, one exception to this rule: character flaws. "Out of principle, you should never compromise on those," he says. "If this person consistently lies, abuses people, or has lousy working habits," that's not likely to change. Besides, he adds, these things tend to come back to haunt you.

Don't succumb to pressure to hire a flawed candidate

Deciding whether or not to hire a candidate who lacks relevant experience in your industry, has an unconventional background, or has some glaring weaknesses is not easy. "We live in a world that is uncertain, ambiguous, and complex," says Fernández-Aráoz. "The fact is, you don't know what the job you're hiring for will look like in a few years," let alone how this candidate will adapt to those changes. When you've got a slate of flawed candidates, he adds, the best you can do is "figure out who is closest to the level required for the job and look at who's the most likely to develop into the role with the right type of support." But don't be impetuous or too quick to give into pressure from your boss to fill the position quickly, says Sullivan. You must weigh the cost of a vacancy with "the cost of hiring a Homer Simpson," especially for a critical, high-risk position. Simply put, don't hire someone who's just "pretty good" for a high-priority job. "It's basic risk management," says Sullivan.

Case Study: Decide What Attributes You Really Want in a Candidate and Assess Interest in Learning

Peter Miller, CEO of OptiNose, a specialty pharmaceutical company, says that inadequate job candidates are the norm, not the exception. "We all have things we're great at, and things we're not so great at," he says. "You won't have a perfect candidate coming through the door and—even after years of development—you won't have a perfect, well-rounded employee."

Earlier in his career, Peter cofounded Take Care Health—a company that manages convenient care clinics and worksite-based health centers—and he needed to hire a chief nurse practitioner officer to lead the nursing organization. Before he and his business partner, Hal Rosenbluth, even reviewed their slate of candidates, they decided on the nonnegotiable attributes of the winning candidate.

"We said: 'What is mission critical to what we're trying to do?' And we realized that we needed someone who could inspire and motivate the other nurse practitioners on the team and someone who had an unrelenting focus on patients."

Peter says they received a great deal of interest in the job. "We had a lot of applications from heads of nurse practitioner organizations and from nurses who were running major parts of hospitals," he recalls.

But the conventional candidates seemed to be missing something. Instead, he was drawn to an unorthodox résumé from Sandy Ryan. Sandy, a former Air Force major, was a nurse in a family clinic. "She had leadership experience—but not in the environment we were looking for," he says. "And she had zero business experience."

Despite these weaknesses, Peter and Hal brought her in for interviews. "I put the job description in front of her, and I said, 'Tell me about what you're going to be exceptional at; and conversely, tell me what you're going to struggle with.'"

Sandy discussed her medical expertise and her patient caretaking abilities. She was also open and honest about her flaws and her lack of business acumen. "Sandy talked about how she was going to go about learning the business and the steps she would take to look for help," says Peter. "It was clear that she was curious, passionate, and driven, and had a capacity to learn."

Peter says that his assistant at the time, Tammy Mc-Cauley, who now serves as chief administrative officer at OptiNose, also provided a favorable opinion of Sandy. "Candidates can be very good at fooling you—they're trying to get the job, but I am always interested to hear how they interacted with Tammy and her impressions," he says. "I don't hire anyone unless Tammy has given her stamp of approval."

Sandy got the job and has been a "star in the industry," says Peter.

Names and identifying details have been changed.

———————

Rebecca Knight is a journalist who writes about all things related to the changing nature of careers and the workplace. Her essays and reported stories have been featured in the *Boston Globe*, *Business Insider*, the *New York Times*, BBC, and the *Christian Science Monitor*. She was shortlisted as a Reuters Institute Fellow at Oxford University in 2023. Earlier in her career, she spent a decade as an editor and reporter in New York, London, and Boston.

CHAPTER 20

Seven Strategies for Better Group Decision-Making

by Torben Emmerling and Duncan Rooders

When you need to hire a new employee, you'll likely need to work with a recruiter and other colleagues in the assessment and selection process. More perspectives will help you make a better recruitment decision, right? Not necessarily. There's no guarantee that more people mean a better outcome. An overreliance on hierarchy, an instinct to prevent dissent, and a desire to preserve harmony leads many groups to fall into *groupthink*.[1]

Misconceived expert opinions can quickly distort a group decision. Individual biases can easily spread

Adapted from content posted on hbr.org, September 22, 2020 (product #H05VFP).

across the group and lead to outcomes far outside individual preferences. And most of these processes occur subconsciously.

This doesn't mean that groups shouldn't make decisions together—especially when it comes to hiring—but you do need to create the right process for doing so. Based on behavioral and decision science research and years of application experience, we have identified seven simple strategies for more effective group decision making:

Keep the group small when you need to make an important decision

While the involvement of many people can help to develop a diverse perspective, large groups are much more likely to make biased decisions. For example, research shows that groups with seven or more members are more susceptible to confirmation bias when it comes to making decisions.[2] The larger the group, the greater the tendency for its members to research and evaluate information in a way that is consistent with preexisting information and beliefs. By keeping the group to between three and five people, a size that people naturally gravitate toward when interacting, you can reduce these negative effects while still benefiting from multiple perspectives.

Choose a heterogenous group over a homogenous one (most of the time)

Various studies have found that groups consisting of individuals with homogeneous opinions and beliefs have a greater tendency toward biased decision-making.[3] Teams that have potentially opposing points of view can more effectively counter biases. However, context matters.[4] When trying to complete complex tasks that require diverse skills and perspectives, such as conducting research and designing processes, heterogeneous groups may substantially outperform homogeneous ones. But in repetitive tasks requiring convergent thinking in structured environments, such as adhering to safety procedures in flying or health care, homogenous groups often do better. As a leader, you need first to understand the nature of the decision you're asking the group to make before you assemble a suitable team.

Appoint a strategic dissenter (or even two)

One way to counter undesirable groupthink tendencies in teams is to appoint a "devil's advocate." This person is tasked with acting as a counterforce to the group's consensus. Research shows that empowering at least one person with the right to challenge the team's decision-making process can lead to significant improvements in decision quality and outcomes.[5] For larger groups with seven or more members, appoint at least two devil's advocates to be sure that a sole strategic dissenter isn't isolated by the rest of the group as a disruptive troublemaker.

Collect opinions independently

The collective knowledge of a group is an advantage only if it's used properly. To get the most out of your team's diverse capabilities, we recommend gathering individual opinions before people share their thoughts within the wider group. You can ask team members to record their ideas independently and anonymously in a shared document, for example. Then ask the group to assess the proposed ideas, again independently and anonymously, without assigning any of the suggestions to particular team members. By following such an iterative process, teams can counter biases and resist groupthink. This process also makes sure that perceived seniority, alleged expertise, or hidden agendas don't play a role in what the group decides to do.

Provide a safe space to speak up

If you want people to share opinions and engage in constructive dissent, they need to feel they can speak up without fear of retribution. Actively encourage reflection on and discussion of divergent opinions, doubts, and experiences in a respectful manner. There are three basic elements required to create a safe space and harness a group's diversity most effectively. First, focus feedback on the decision or discussed strategy, not on the individual. Second, express comments as suggestions, not as mandates. Third, express feedback in a way that shows you empathize with and appreciate the individuals working toward your joint goal.

Don't overrely on experts

Experts can help groups make more informed decisions. However, blind trust in expert opinions can make a group susceptible to biases and distort the outcome.[6]

Research demonstrates that making them part of the decision-making can sway the team to adapt their opinions to those of the expert or make overconfident judgments.[7] Therefore, invite experts to provide their opinion on a clearly defined topic, and position them as informed outsiders in relation to the group.

Share collective responsibility

Finally, the outcome of a decision may be influenced by elements as simple as the choice of the group's messenger. We often observe a single individual being responsible for selecting suitable group members, organizing the agenda, and communicating the results. When this is the case, individual biases can easily influence the decision of an entire team. Research shows that such negative tendencies can be effectively counteracted if different roles are assigned to different group members based on their expertise.[8] Moreover, all members should feel accountable for the group's decision-making process and its final outcome. One way to do that is to ask the team to sign a joint responsibility statement at the outset, leading to a more balanced distribution of power and a more open exchange of ideas.

Of course, following these steps doesn't guarantee a great recruitment decision and ultimately a great hire. However, the better the quality of the decision-making process and the interaction between the group members, the greater your chances selecting someone who positively contributes to your organization.

Torben Emmerling is the founder and managing partner of Affective Advisory and the author of the D.R.I.V.E. framework for behavioral insights in strategy and public policy. He is a founding member and nonexecutive director on the board of the Global Association of Applied Behavioural Scientists (GAABS) and a seasoned lecturer, keynote speaker, and author in behavioral science, decision science, and applied consumer psychology.

Duncan Rooders is the CEO of a Single Family Office and a strategic adviser to Affective Advisory. He is a former B747 pilot, a graduate of Harvard Business School's Owner/President Management program, and the founder of Behavioural Science for Business (BSB), advising several international organizations in strategic and team and financial decision-making.

NOTES

1. Irving Janis, "Groupthink," in *A First Look at Communication Theory*, ed. Em Griffin (New York: McGrawHill, 1991), 235–246.

2. Dieter Frey, Stefan Schulz-Hardt, and Dagmar Stahlberg, "Information Seeking Among Individuals and Groups and Possible Consequences for Decision Making in Business and Politics," in *Understanding Group Behavior*, vol. 2, *Small Group Processes and Interpersonal Relations*, ed. Erich H. Witte and James H. Davis (Mahwah, NJ: Lawrence Erlbaum Associates, 1996), 211–225.

3. Stefan Schulz-Hardt, Dieter Frey, Carsten Lüthgens, and Serge Moscovici, "Biased Information Search in Group Decision Making," *Journal of Personality and Social Psychology* 78, no. 4 (2000): 655–669. https://doi.org/10.1037/0022-3514.78.4.655.

4. Norbert L. Kerr, Robert J. MacCoun, and Geoffrey P. Kramer, "When Are N Heads Better (or Worse) Than One?: Biased Judgment in Individuals Versus Groups," in *Understanding Group Behavior*, vol. 2, *Small Group Processes and Interpersonal Relations*, ed. Erich H. Witte and James H. Davis (Mahwah, NJ: Lawrence Erlbaum Associates, 1996), 105–136.

5. David M. Schweiger, William R. Sandberg, and James W. Ragan, "Group Approaches for Improving Strategic Decision Making: A Comparative Analysis of Dialectical Inquiry, Devil's Advocacy, and Consensus," *Academy of Management Journal* 29, no. 1 (1986): 51–71, https://doi.org/10.5465/255859.

6. Dilek Önkal, Paul Goodwin, and Mary Thomson et al., "The Relative Influence of Advice from Human Experts and Statistical Methods on Forecast Adjustments," *Journal of Behavioral Decision Making*, 22 (2009): 390–409, https://doi.org/10.1002/bdm.637.

7. Andreas Mojzisch, Stefan Schulz-Hardt, Rudolf Kerschreiter, and Dieter Frey, "Combined Effects of Knowledge About Others' Opinions and Anticipation of Group Discussion on Confirmatory Information Search," *Small Group Research* 39, no. 2 (2008): 203–223, https://doi.org/10.1177/1046496408315983.

8. Cass R. Sunstein and Reid Hastie, "Making Dumb Groups Smarter," *Harvard Business Review*, December 2014.

CHAPTER 21

A Scorecard for Making Better Hiring Decisions

by Ben Dattner

Most companies and individuals make less-than-stellar investments in human capital, particularly when using interviews to evaluate candidates. Why? Because people are biased, emotional, and inconsistent when interviewing.

Using the model of detection theory, there are four basic scenarios for interviewing and hiring. The first is that a "good" candidate is hired, constituting a "hit." If the "good" candidate is not hired, this is a "miss." In the

---

Adapted from content posted on hbr.org, February 4, 2016 (product #H02NFH).

event that a "bad" candidate is not hired, this is a "correct rejection." And if a "bad" candidate is hired, this is a "false positive."

Interviewers tend to be most concerned with trying to avoid false positives, as hiring a candidate who doesn't work out can be highly problematic. It's rare that an interviewer ever finds out about a miss (e.g., that a candidate who was not hired became very successful somewhere else). Your "hit rate" can be calculated by the ratio of your hits and correct rejections to your misses and false positives.

How can you improve your hiring hit rate? An interview scorecard can provide a quantitative basis for comparison between interviewers, enabling you to validate your perceptions with your colleagues and learn where your ratings may be outside of the norm. By correlating your predictions with candidates' actual performance on the job, you can also get quantitative feedback about your accuracy at assessing different criteria. Only by developing awareness of our own evaluative interview biases is it possible to correct them.

To create an interview scorecard, write down ratings along five or so applicable criteria (see table 21-1), and then periodically revisit them. Discuss and debate your candidate ratings with colleagues to assess and improve your individual and collective accuracy. You might learn that you are good at assessing technical ability, but less accurate in your evaluation of leadership skills. Or that a colleague is too lenient on some criteria and too stringent on others.

TABLE 21-1

Interview scorecard

Candidate name _____

Position interviewed for _____

Date _____

CRITERION	INTERVIEW RATING (1-5)	PERFORMANCE RATING AFTER HIRE (1-5)	GAP	COMMENTS/ LESSONS LEARNED
1. Technical ability				
2. Leadership skills				
3. Interpersonal/ team skills				
4. Presentation skills				
5. Organizational citizenship				

OVERALL STRENGTHS: **OVERALL CONCERNS:**   **WHAT WOULD HELP THIS CANDIDATE BE MOST SUCCESSFUL IN THE ROLE?**

Source: Dattner Consulting, LLC.

219

When used properly and consistently, interview score-cards help level the playing field for candidates, create a quantitative basis for comparison and validation, and enable you and your organization to make better hiring decisions over time.

Ben Dattner is an executive coach and organizational development consultant, and the founder of New York City-based Dattner Consulting, LLC.

CHAPTER 22

Why You Should Invest in Unconventional Talent

by Debbie Ferguson and Fredrick "Flee" Lee

What do an administrative assistant, exercise physiologist, and music composition major have in common? They are all among our top hires for software developer roles.

Many stellar engineers have no formal certifications or degrees; some didn't go to college. We believe that there's no single "best" route to a role. Often, less-traveled

---

Adapted from content posted on hbr.org, May 25, 2021 (product #H06DVA).

roads can provide invaluable experience and unexpected perspectives.

We've walked these unconventional paths ourselves as a self-taught hacker and a first-generation college graduate, respectively. We've worked at companies where we were the "only" on a team—the only Black engineer (Flee), the only trans engineer (Debbie), or the only woman (Debbie)—and we've been told, implicitly and explicitly, that we don't fit the mold. We've been in the room when hiring committees passed up qualified candidates in favor of those with more traditional pedigrees.

Those experiences fueled our passion to hire differently and to encourage other leaders to do the same.

The importance of building diverse organizations has been well established. Diversity is linked to greater innovation and performance; McKinsey found that more diverse companies had higher profits than their more homogeneous counterparts.[1]

In contrast, a lack of diversity can lead to convergent thinking. People who share training and experiences tend to reach a consensus faster because they view problems the same way.[2] However, the long-term impact is less beneficial, resulting in narrower thinking and products that don't meet their potential.

Building teams with different skill sets and life experiences requires intention. By designing inclusive hiring practices—and letting go of the notion that there's one ideal candidate type for a role—we can create more opportunities for a range of candidates who are more than capable. Here's how.

Focus on potential rather than pedigree

We asked developers at Gusto to talk about their backgrounds and noticed a common theme: Many discovered a passion for building software through a mix of self-study, experimentation, and formal classes. Others found their love of engineering through seemingly unrelated jobs, including being a paralegal and a video editor.

We both began our careers with different tool sets than we use today. Many, if not most, skills can be taught on the job; what matters is the desire and core capabilities to succeed. Jobs are changing so rapidly that adaptable learners are in high demand.[3] Many top companies, including Google, Apple, and Bank of America, now focus less on "official" qualifications—many are no longer requiring traditional degrees—and we're excited to see this trend continue.[4]

The truth is that the skills that seem ideal for a role today may no longer even be a fit in a year. When you're screening and interviewing candidates, look for ways to explore the capabilities that will enable the individual to thrive as everything around them changes. Consider asking questions like the following:

- **What were you doing the last time you looked at a clock and realized you had lost all track of time?** An open-ended question like this can help you uncover intellectual curiosity and understand what motivates someone.

- **Describe a project you're proud of that involved working closely with other people.** Give candidates the opportunity to demonstrate self-awareness and teamwork; for example, by discussing how they raised up their team and vice versa.

Look for the sparkles in your talent pool

Unconventional hiring is an exercise in holding up diamonds to the light. You're training your eye to spot what glitters, which might be someone's volunteer or advocacy work, music, writing, or an insightful social media thread.

One of our most prolific interviewers bases her questions on a candidate's LinkedIn profile—but not the section you might think. She jumps to interests and the people they follow, rather than starting with education, endorsements, or even experience. Those sparks can be more telling than a job title.

Events and contests can also help you expand your talent pool to people who may not yet see themselves as experienced professionals. We find coding competitions to be rich sources of passionate and unconventional talent. One of our best hires for security engineering was a financial analyst who excelled in a cybersecurity contest. In these contests, sparkling doesn't necessarily mean winning. Runners-up often make strong candidates because they're less focused on rushing to complete a challenge and more interested in methodically solving a problem.

Help unconventional candidates envision themselves at your company

Recruiting nontraditional hires sometimes involves convincing someone they can flourish in a role they can't yet imagine. Job descriptions, your company's LinkedIn profile, and your website's careers section are all venues to reinforce your culture and ethos. Use those opportunities to authentically describe what it's like to work at your company, then consider how those descriptions may resonate with candidates with different career experiences and backgrounds. For example, look for ways to minimize jargon; insider language could discourage candidates from applying, even if they have a real shot.

Another way to welcome unconventional applicants is to paint the big picture of a role rather than a checklist of specialized skills, degrees, or years of experience. When crafting job descriptions, we focus on what the candidate can expect to do day-to-day and what we're looking for at a high level, such as an "interest in complex product development problems." If we mention specific programming languages, we'll clarify that you don't need to know them because there will be training on the job.

When writing job descriptions, focus on the essential components of a given role. For every requirement or responsibility, keep asking why it's crucial. For example, when we're writing the job description for an engineering role, we could require that applicants have experience with Amazon Web Services, the cloud service provider we use—but why? We need engineers who understand cloud computing, and the security needs and scale that come with it. That experience with cloud services is essential, but a specific provider is not. We need someone who knows how to drive a car, not someone who knows how to drive a particular make and model. The job description should reflect that; otherwise, we narrow the applicant pool unnecessarily.

With artificial intelligence likely to reshape nearly every task and job over the coming years, your employees must be resilient and adaptable. During interviews, ask for examples of where a candidate had to handle a significant and unexpected change. Listen to whether the candidate leaned into the challenge, took ownership, and worked through options to achieve a good outcome. Often, unconventional candidates have faced and overcome a variety of challenges in their careers and lives.

We encourage every hiring manager to think beyond the confines of traditional hiring. Prepare for new hires who shake up your worldview and challenge assumptions about career paths. Continue investing in their growth. Together, chart an unconventional course toward the destination: an inclusive workplace for extraordinary talent.

———————

Debbie Ferguson is CEO and founder of GratiSports. Previous roles include vice president at Gusto, senior engineering executive at Google, an early leader at Facebook, and founder and CEO of Ignite Logic.

Fredrick "Flee" Lee has over 20 years of experience leading global information security and privacy efforts at major financial services companies and technology startups, including as Chief Security Officer at Square and most recently as Chief Security Officer and Head of IT at Gusto. Flee is currently CISO at Reddit. He oversees Reddit's Privacy and Security teams responsible for identifying and mitigating risks and challenges around information security, privacy, and compliance. Flee is a proud Southerner, raised in Mississippi, and holds a bachelor's degree in computer engineering from the University of Oklahoma. In his spare time, Flee enjoys rock climbing, snowboarding, mountain biking, road cycling, and powerlifting, and is a passionate Redditor, lurking in r/MMA, r/Awwducational, r/selfhosted, and r/netsec.

NOTES

1. Sundiatu Dixon-Fyle, Kevin Dolan, Dame Vivian Hunt, and Sara Prince, "Diversity Wins: How Inclusion Matters," mckinsey.com, May 19, 2020, https://www.mckinsey.com/featured-insights/diversity-and-inclusion/diversity-wins-how-inclusion-matters.

2. Richard P. Larrick, "Broaden the Decision Frame to Make Effective Decisions," in *Handbook of Principles of Organizational Behavior: Indispensable Knowledge for Evidence-Based Management*, 2nd edition, ed. Edwin A. Locke (Chichester, UK: John Wiley & Sons Ltd, 2009), https://sites.duke.edu/larrick/files/2014/09/2009-Larrick-Handbook-of-Principles-of-Org-Behavior.pdf.

3. Darren Shimkus, "Why Your Next Hire Should Be an Adaptable Learner," HR Dive, August 22, 2017, https://www.hrdive.com/news/why-your-next-hire-should-be-an-adaptable-learner/503190/.

4. Glassdoor Team, "33 Companies Actively Hiring Right Now," Glassdoor, July 3, 2024, https://www.glassdoor.com/blog/companies-actively-hiring/.

CHAPTER 23

Don't Hire a Former Employee Before Asking These Questions

by Marlo Lyons

Many employees are on the move, looking for that next opportunity. Perhaps they want a bigger challenge, more money, or believe they need to leave their current company to advance their career. But what if they leave your company and realize the new opportunity wasn't as great as they thought, or they left years ago, gained new skills, and now want to come back? Should you hire them?

Adapted from content posted on hbr.org, January 26, 2022 (product #H06TT6).

Rehiring a former employee, known as a *boomerang*, may seem like the easy answer because they already know the company culture, business nuances, and people, but there are several reasons why they might not be the right person for the job. Here are five questions managers should ask themselves before hiring a former employee.

Am I hiring the boomerang employee because it seems like the easy option?

The employee knows the company, but is the new job exactly the same as the one they left? Most employees will come back to an employer for a different or more senior role. Consider how they'll adjust to a different role and whether their colleagues will see them as capable of that higher-level position. Check in with their previous manager (if applicable), HR, and cross-functional stakeholders not only about whether the employee should be considered for rehire, but also about their soft skills and ability to adjust to new and dynamic situations. This will help you foresee any roadblocks to the boomerang's success in the new role.

Then think about how they'll fit into the culture of your team. Is it the same team, or has it changed or grown since they left? If it's a new team, how will the boomerang fit in with the current employees? Will they be managing any former colleagues who were previously peers? And how will that impact the team dynamics? What will you need to do to ensure a smooth transition for the boomerang and the team?

Finally, do you equate "easier" with "no ramp time?" You may think the boomerang doesn't need much on-boarding, especially if they're returning to the same team, but companies, teams, and processes grow and change, and boomerangs deserve the same amount of ramp time as any new employee. If they get back into the swing of things quickly, then great!

Does the boomerang bring the right skills and capabilities to advance the business?

You're familiar with the skills and capabilities the employee had before they left the company. What new skills and experience have they gained since leaving? Do those skills match the job description and help advance the business, or are their current and previous skills obsolete compared to where the company is headed? Making sure the boomerang has the skills that fit the job responsibilities and business needs is critical to moving the company forward.

Is unconscious bias influencing me?

When employees leave a company, they often keep in touch with former colleagues. If you've remained friendly with the boomerang employee and talked to them about a role you're hiring for, there's a chance unconscious bias contributed to how you designed the job description. Consider whether you drafted the job description objectively or wrote it to match the potential boomerang's experience and level, which might not match the business needs.

Unconscious bias could also influence how you manage this friend-employee. Being a "frien-ager"—a friend who becomes a manager—can lead to inequity on the team. What will you do to combat unconscious bias in promotions, performance reviews, and overall strategic conversations?

When a high school friend hired me at NBC, we had a detailed conversation about our expectations as a manager and employee. I was fortunate, because he was a great boss and provided ample feedback and guidance. If I saw him and his family on the weekends, we did not discuss work or any employee; and when in the office, we didn't discuss any personal information outside of a group setting. It was a delicate balance that required a level of maturity to not make others feel excluded from "inside jokes" or make them feel that their relationships with the manager were any less meaningful than mine.

The best way to combat unconscious bias is to understand what it is, acknowledge it can exist, and listen to all employees (including the boomerang) equally. A transparent, detailed conversation with all team members about how you expect to behave as their manager and what you expect of them—to tell you if you faltered in your efforts to manage fairly—will help your employees feel empowered to discuss any perceived unfairness and will combat divisiveness within your team.

Have expectations of the "what" and the "how" changed since the employee left?

Your company may have grown or changed since the former employee left, and that means the expectations of your team have changed. When they previously worked for your company, the boomerang may have exceeded all expectations on deliverables and been beloved by everyone who knew them. But if the expectations are different or higher now, will they be able to deliver as effectively as before?

Communicate any different or higher expectations to the boomerang throughout the hiring process. They need to be able to determine if the role is right for them and whether they can be successful based on the changed expectations. Without this transparency, you won't be able to have a mutual understanding of what success looks like in the role.

Will I be able to provide opportunities that ensure retention long term?

As a hiring manager, it's your job to understand what's important to your employees (in other words, their values). If a former employee wants to come back, it's important to have an honest conversation about what they're looking for, why the role could be fulfilling for them, and what it will take to keep them engaged long term. For example, if the employee left to gain new skills, how will you ensure they can use those skills in this new role? What else do they want to learn, and can you provide that opportunity? If the employee left because of a lack of connection with their previous boss, will they be able to engage with you successfully? If they left for a higher title or more money, will they feel stifled again after a short period of time without a promotion or jump in salary? Without understanding the employee's values, it will be hard to provide opportunities that ensure long-term retention.

Boomerangs can provide great value to an organization based on their previous experience and the new perspectives and skills gained at another employer. It's up to managers to ensure the boomerang will be able to bring that value in the new role.

———————

Marlo Lyons is a career, executive, and team coach, as well as the award-winning author of *Wanted—A New Career: The Definitive Playbook for Transitioning to a New Career or Finding Your Dream Job*. You can reach her at marlolyonscoaching.com.

Make an Offer or Reject Candidates

CHAPTER 24

Negotiate an Offer That Works

by Michael Schaerer, Martin Schweinsberg, and Roderick Swaab

Negotiation experts have long advised a win-win approach focused on creating mutual value. This approach effectively turns counterparties into collaborators instead of adversaries, pooling their creative resources to "expand the pie" rather than fighting over the size of their respective slices. Not only does this generate more financial value for everyone, but it also has interpersonal benefits: Business relationships are stronger after the negotiation if all parties walk away happy with the outcome. (See table 24-1 for a quick refresh of the basic negotiation process.)

Adapted from "How to Play 'Friendly Hardball' in a Negotiation" on hbr.org, June 30, 2020 (product #H05PPG).

TABLE 24-1

The negotiation process

Every negotiation involves different players, interests, and goals. Despite those differences, most negotiations follow the four phases shown here. Once you understand the process and strategies for each phase, you can adapt your approach to individual situations.

Phases of negotiation	What's involved
1. Prepare to negotiate	• Identify the type and scope of the negotiation. • Establish and improve your position. • Identify your own interests. • Assess the other party's position. • Identify your counterpart's interests. • Identify the zone of possible agreement. • Plan your opening move and contingency moves.
2. Conduct the negotiation, including offers and counteroffers	• Set the stage and tone. • Use your planned strategies. • Continually evaluate what's happening.
3. Finalize the agreement	• Prevent errors, and manage your emotions. • Handle impasses. • Close the deal. • Evaluate the outcome.
4. Fulfill the agreement	• Carry out the agreement. • Meet your commitments. • Capture and share what you learned.

Source: Adapted from "Understand Negotiation," Harvard ManageMentor, https://hbp.myhbp.org/hmm12/content/negotiating/understand_negotiation.html.

This win-win mindset works well for negotiations with multiple issues, since having more than one issue to discuss gives negotiators flexibility to explore priorities and make mutually beneficial trade-offs. However, a win-win approach is considered to be unsuitable for negotiations with only one issue that cannot be transformed into multi-issue negotiations, which is sometimes the case when negotiating salary or rent. (See table 24-2 for a quick overview of single- versus multi-issue negotiations.) In such negotiations, we often assume that one party's gains are the other party's losses, and the more you push your counterparty, the less satisfied they will be with the deal. Common wisdom therefore suggests that the best you can do is weigh your desired financial result against the importance of preserving a positive relationship and decide how aggressively to negotiate accordingly.

TABLE 24-2

Identify the type of negotiation: Single- versus multi-issue negotiations

Before you begin bargaining, you need to know what kind of negotiation you're engaging in. This knowledge will influence your strategy and the choices you make. The two main types are single-issue negotiation, also known as "distributive" or "win-lose" negotiation, and multi-issue negotiation, also known as "integrative" or "win-win" negotiation. Although negotiators should attempt to transform a single-issue negotiation into a multi-issue negotiation to create actual and perceived flexibility, it may not always be possible to do so.

Characteristic	Single-issue negotiations	Multi-issue negotiations
Number of issues involved	One	Several
Outcome	Win-lose	Win-win
Motivation	Individual gain	Joint and individual gain
Interests	Opposed	Different value and priority placed on issues
Duration	Short-term	Short- or long-term
Ability to make trade-offs	Not flexible	Flexible
Solution	Not creative	Creative

Source: Adapted from "Prepare to Negotiate," Harvard ManageMentor, https://hbp.myhbp.org/hmm12/content/negotiating/prepare_to_negotiate.html.

But research shows that there is another option. In a paper for the *Journal of Experimental Social Psychology* we coauthored with Nico Thornley, we found that even single-issue negotiations can have a win-win outcome if you frame them in a careful—and counterintuitive—way: By contrasting your offers against the *least your counterparty is willing to accept* (aka their *walkaway price*), you're likely to obtain a more favorable counteroffer and leave both parties happier.[1]

In a series of three experiments, participants conducted several negotiations with variations of the question: "How does my offer compare to the minimum price you would be willing to accept?" We found that this framing led other negotiators to not only make less ambitious counteroffers but also to report greater satisfaction than those who were asked to frame their offers against a target price or weren't asked to use any framing techniques.

Why does this work? In negotiations, we compare offers to reference points—or *anchors*, as they are sometimes called. How we feel about a given dollar amount depends on what we're comparing it to. Framing an offer by asking your counterparty to compare it to their walkaway price instead of their target price anchors their expectations, leading them to think about your offer as a gain rather than a loss and thus increasing the likelihood that they will be pleased rather than disappointed with the outcome.

Despite its effectiveness in our studies, this framing technique is rarely adopted in the real world: When we observed 152 simulated job negotiations between MBA students, we found that only four negotiators naturally used a strategy resembling the walkaway-price framing approach. We subsequently launched three negotiation exercises in which we asked participants (groups of MBA students, undergraduates, and working professionals) to imagine themselves in the role of a recruiter who had recently interviewed a great candidate and now had to negotiate their salary.

They were told that they had to choose between using either walkaway-price framing ("My offer is ___. How does my offer compare to the highest offer you have received from another company?") or target framing ("My offer is ___. How does my offer compare to your ideal salary?"). The overwhelming majority in all samples opted for target framing. The participants told us that they did so because they were afraid that walkaway-price framing would be detrimental from a relational perspective: They felt that it ran the risk of being interpreted as an impolite, offensive move (despite the fact that our studies show walkaway-price framing is actually less likely to leave the counterpart dissatisfied than the more intuitive target-price framing method).

A fourth and final study revealed an important limitation of the walkaway-price technique: Its effectiveness is diminished when the counterparty already has a strong alternative offer. Participants with a strong alternative responded to walkaway-price framing with counteroffers that were comparable to the target-framing condition and *more* ambitious than the no-framing condition. Moreover, walkaway-price framing also resulted in lower satisfaction rates when participants were told that they had a strong alternative offer. Together, these findings suggest that the walkaway-price framing technique is very effective when negotiating with someone who doesn't already have an attractive offer, but if your counterparty does have a strong existing offer, that will render this approach ineffective.

The walkaway-price framing technique will be especially effective when your counterparty has either no alternatives or only weak alternatives. It's important to keep in mind that if your counterparty does have a strong alternative offer, the walkaway-price method could backfire. However, if you're confident that your counterparty's existing options are limited, this strategy can be a simple though counterintuitive way to play hardball in your negotiation while maintaining a positive business relationship.

THINGS TO KEEP IN MIND WHEN USING WALKAWAY-PRICE FRAMING

- Do your homework. Before starting the conversation, figure out the "bargaining zone" for your negotiation, or the area between the various parties' baseline expectations. If you make an offer without considering the bargaining zone, you're unlikely to be successful—no matter how you frame that offer.

- You should also do your best to determine whether there are any preexisting offers on the table that might impact your counterparty's walkaway price and adjust your negotiation strategy accordingly. The more attractive your counterparty's alternative offers, the less advantageous walkaway-price framing is likely to be.

- Before anchoring your counterparty, determine whether the issue in question is truly isolated, or may have implications for other issues. A premature offer pertaining to a single issue, even one that's in your favor, may hinder you from finding trade-offs between issues that could create even more shared value.

Michael Schaerer is an associate professor of organizational behavior and human resources at Singapore Management University's Lee Kong Chian School of Business.

Martin Schweinsberg is an associate professor of organizational behavior at ESMT Berlin.

Roderick Swaab is the INSEAD chaired professor of leadership and conflict resolution and codirector of the Negotiation and Conflict Management Collaborative.

NOTE

1. Michael Schaerer, Martin Schweinsberg, Nico Thornley, and Roderick I. Swaab, "Win-Win in Distributive Negotiations: The Economic and Relational Benefits of Strategic Offer Framing," *Journal of Experimental Social Psychology* 87 (2020): 1–8, https://doi.org/10.1016/j.jesp.2019.103943.

CHAPTER 25

How to Write a Good Rejection Letter

by Sarah Green Carmichael

Rejection letters aren't easy for any of us to write. Whether you're telling a job candidate that they didn't make the next round, an entrepreneur that you're not going to fund their project, or a vendor that you no longer need their services, these are emails most of us dread crafting. Because it's unpleasant, too many of us put it off or don't do it at all, essentially letting our silence do the talking. That's a missed opportunity (and rude). Though painful, rejection has benefits: Research by

---

Adapted from "Writing a Rejection Letter (with Samples)" on hbr.org, October 3, 2016 (product #H03620).

Linus Dahlander at ESMT and Henning Piezunka at INSEAD has found, for example, that when organizations take the time to explicitly reject (rather than just passively ignore) crowdsourced ideas, it both increases the quality of the ideas they're being offered and increases the engagement of the crowd.

If there's one thing that I've learned in a decade at *Harvard Business Review*—during which I've rejected literally thousands of ideas, pitches, and drafts—it's that a quick "no" is better than a long "maybe."

Writing a Basic Rejection Letter

Writing good rejections does take a bit of time—especially at first. But one of the benefits of learning to write a good rejection letter is that it forces you to think clearly about what it is that you want from other people, and what it is that your organization really needs.

Rejection letters need not be long, and the reason you give for the rejection need not be super-detailed. If you don't have much of a relationship with the person—you never met them, maybe just traded some emails—the entire letter might be only a few lines. I looked back at some rejection letters I sent and realized that I usually follow a pretty simple format:

1. Say thanks.

2. Deliver the news.

3. Give the main reason.

4. Offer hope.

For example:

[Their name],

Thanks for making the time to talk with me last week. While I enjoyed our conversation, I think we need someone with more hands-on project management experience for this role. I hope you find the right job for you in the near future.

[Your name]

If you can't think of any hope to offer at the end, then don't. "Do not say anything that will give the recipient the impression that the door is still open," Jocelyn Glei advises in her email writing guide, *Unsubscribe*. "Such clarity and finality can feel cruel, but adding additional language to 'soften the blow' only serves to create false hope. Say your piece and sign off." False hope is crueler than no hope. False hope just encourages the other person to waste more of their time, and yours.

Writing a Detailed Rejection Letter

But what if the person was really close to being a good fit, and you might want to work with them in the future? Or you have more of a relationship with them? In those cases, the above message is probably too cold and too vague. When rejecting people I want to encourage, I keep the format much the same but am generally *much* more detailed in my reason for rejecting and more explicit in encouraging the person to try again. (Dahlander and Piezunka found that providing an explanation about why an idea was being rejected bolstered the beneficial effects of rejection—e.g., motivation and idea quality.)

I also often end with a question to try to signal that I'm genuinely interested—not just making an empty, softening-the-blow promise. For example:

[Their name],

Thanks for making the time to talk with me last week. I'm sorry to say that your candidacy did not make it to the next round; we've had a very competitive pool for this position. At this point, our organization really needs someone with more project management experience. However, I really enjoyed our conversation and think you could be a good fit here in the right role. Please do keep in touch—and is it OK with you if I let you know about roles that open up that might be a better fit?

All the best,
[Your name]

The more specific you are about the way you reject someone, the more information you give them. A smart rejectee will use this information to come back with a stronger case the next time. I've actually had a few people thank me for rejection letters I wrote to them because it gave them the kind of concrete, specific feedback they needed to get better results in their future attempts. It's a good reminder that people do value receiving criticism, even though most of us dread giving it.

Writing a Rejection Letter When You Disagree with the Decision

It's especially tough to pass along a rejection decision that you disagree with. Maybe you fought hard for a job candidate everyone else was unimpressed by, or championed the cause of a vendor that the executive committee thought was too expensive. I know I've argued for articles that other editors thought weren't ready for prime time. It's not a good feeling.

When this happens, it's tempting to hide behind passive voice or other people—e.g., "It has been decided that we won't be pursuing this" or "The bigwigs have decided to go in a different direction." Resist that temptation. It's not any easier to get rejected in that fashion, and writing that way undercuts your authority as a decision-maker.

If you're the one issuing a rejection, own the rejection. It's fair to say something like, "After a lot of discussion and back-and-forth, we've decided X" or "It was a really hard decision, but we've ultimately decided Y." But say "we," not "they."

A rejection letter in which you're hiding behind a nebulous "they" inhibits your ability to give useful feedback. It also makes your organization look fractious or contentious, which undermines other people's desire to work with you in the future.

Delivering bad news is tough, and in different companies or cultures, these examples may sound either overly harsh or too nice. You'll need to find your own language depending on the context and the culture. That said, remember: Don't soften the blow just for the sake of sparing pain. False kindness just gives people false hope. And there's nothing kind about that.

––––––––

Sarah Green Carmichael is a former executive editor at *Harvard Business Review*.

CHAPTER 26

Why You Should Interview People After They Turn Down a Job with Your Company

by Ben Dattner

Successfully competing for top talent involves both selling jobs to the best candidates and retaining the highest-performing incumbents. To be seen as an employer of choice with a compelling value proposition for employees, many companies measure turnover and conduct exit

Adapted from content posted on hbr.org, August 1, 2016 (product #H031A7).

interviews with departing employees to gather feedback about the experiences people had working there and the reasons why they're leaving. But a less common practice is to track how many people turn down job offers at your company, and an even less common practice is to actually gather feedback from candidates who receive offers but don't accept them. Like "exit interviews" these "declined offer" interviews can yield a lot of information about your own organization as well as valuable data about your industry and competitors.

While academic institutions often gather feedback from students who are accepted but do not matriculate in order to improve student recruitment and retention and to better compete with rival institutions, doing so with job candidates in a systematic and consistent manner is rare in the corporate world. As with other kinds of selling and marketing, you may learn as much, if not more, from the feedback of customers who choose not to buy as you learn from those who do.

If you don't solicit private feedback from people whom you've interviewed (and even if you do), they may provide unsolicited public feedback on websites such as Glassdoor about their experiences being interviewed at your organization. "Declined offer" interviews and feedback can also give you advance warning about factors that may cause your offer rate to decline, enabling you to take proactive steps to prevent it from happening.

The feedback that candidates provide can fall into several categories. There may be some factors that are completely out of your control as hiring manager—for example, if the candidate ultimately decides to pursue another career path or work in a different industry or geographic location. Other feedback may be within your company's control, but difficult to change in the short term, such as the title or level of the job in question or the compensation and benefits package being offered.

However, the feedback that is most likely to be useful and within your control is also likely to be the most sensitive and difficult for the candidate to feel comfortable sharing. It might be hard for a candidate to openly tell you or your human resources partner that they thought you were unfriendly or unfocused, that some interviewers conveyed a low level of enthusiasm about working at your organization, that there were too many interviewers in the mix, or that different interviewers seemed to convey divergent ideas about the company's strategy and plans, the level of authority or responsibilities in the role, the key challenges of the role, or what would be necessary for success.

It's helpful to collect feedback anonymously through online surveys or email; via a third party such as an external search, consulting, or research firm; or through an internal market research, branding, or analytics department that is outside of both the hiring area and human resources. By gathering feedback through one of these channels, candidates can be sufficiently candid and specific about their experiences and suggestions without having concerns about burning any bridges.

Inform candidates who decline offers that their participation in a "declined offer interview" will be much appreciated, that there are no hard feelings, and that when requested and feasible, their individual feedback can remain confidential or anonymous. Knowing that your organization will keep the door open for other potential future opportunities and is committed to continuously improving its competitiveness as an employer might also encourage candidates to participate and provide their honest perspectives.

Here are some questions that you can and should ask the candidates who got away:

- What did you see as the potential positive aspects of the role and/or working at our organization?

- What were your concerns about the role and/or working at our organization?

- What were the most important factors in the decision you made?

- What feedback or suggestions do you have about your interviews, interviewers, the interview process itself, or how we could have improved your overall experience as a candidate?

- Can you provide any observations about, or feedback or suggestions for the hiring manager, HR, or the organization overall?

- What additional feedback or suggestions can you provide about how we might present a more compelling value proposition to candidates like you in the future?

This kind of feedback can provide ample opportunities for your organization to develop theories about how to improve your processes, branding, and candidate experience. It's important to understand, though, that personal sensitivities and organizational politics will inevitably influence the hypotheses that people develop, the interpretations they make, the conclusions they reach and the "stories" they tell themselves and others. As hiring manager, you may believe that HR didn't manage the candidate's timing and logistics properly, while HR may believe that your interviewing skills aren't strong or that you're not a dynamic enough speaker to present the company well. Both you and HR may believe that the CEO should have cleared their calendar to meet with the candidate earlier in the process.

These varying interpretations and perspectives mean it's important to frame this feedback collection in a positive, forward-looking way, to keep an open mind, and to ask candidates who received but did not accept offers open-ended and non-leading questions to get their true impressions and feelings. If they decided to take a different offer, or to remain at their current job, it's helpful to know which criteria they used in making their decision, especially if it was a hard choice for them to make.

With HR, you can also compare and contrast feedback from those who did not take offers with the feedback from those who did and try to ascertain which controllable factors might make the difference in the decision-making process of future candidates that your organization wants to attract. For example, your organization may realize it needs to train hiring managers to be more friendly and focused during interviews, or to ask more relevant job-related questions. Or you can work with HR to seek out a more diverse and enthusiastic group of interviewers who may also represent the organization better to different kinds of candidates and potentially build more positive interpersonal chemistry with them.

It's not easy for any hiring manager, HR department or organization to confront rejection and deal with it constructively. However, by having the courage and discipline to gather, learn from, and productively act on the open and honest feedback of candidates who got away, you and your colleagues can enhance your employment brand, sell your value proposition more effectively than your organization's rivals, improve the candidate experience, and boost your offer acceptance rate in the future.

————————

Ben Dattner is an executive coach and organizational development consultant, and the founder of New York City-based Dattner Consulting, LLC.

When You Can't Find a Match

CHAPTER 27

Sometimes Hiring Nobody Is Better Than Hiring Just Anybody

by Margaret M. Luciano and Maximilian K. Watson

As the exodus of workers referred to as the "great resignation" tolls, "now hiring" signs are ubiquitous. These vacant positions often increase the burden on existing staff members, creating the potential for dissatisfaction, burnout, and even more vacancies. Yet the temptation to hire anyone willing to take the job should be tempered by the many potential consequences of making a bad hire.[1]

Adapted from "When Hiring Nobody Is Better Than Hiring Just Anybody" on hbr.org, December 6, 2021 (product #H06Q3C).

So, if both hiring no one or hiring "just anyone" can be harmful, how do managers know whether it's better to take a chance on a non-ideal candidate or keep a position vacant until they're able to find a better one? Beyond the traditional recommendations of finding someone who is minimally qualified, we've found that the following four traits have the biggest impact on teams. Here's what to look out for—and how to support your current employees in the meantime while you're short-staffed.

Reliability

The past few years have made flexibility a priority for many workers. Despite the fact that widespread work from home has been largely successful, many managers still conflate flexibility with reliability.

Flexibility (e.g., needing to work a 3–2–2 schedule, having every Friday off work, etc.) is predictable and thus easier to manage than unreliability (e.g., frequently calling out of work at the last minute, failing to complete tasks, etc.).[2] During the recruitment process, applicants will often express flexibility-related requests, but of course are unlikely to reveal reliability issues unprompted. First, brush up on your reference-checking skills (including backdoor references) to try to screen out unreliable workers.[3] Second, as you prepare for interviews, consider including behavioral questions that might provide clues—for example, "Tell me about a time when you faced unexpected events and how you managed them."

We all have unexpected situations come up, but in general, adaptable and resilient individuals are more likely to be reliable. If the candidate is likely to be reliable and the team's workflow can accommodate any flexibility requests they may have, keep them under consideration. If not, consider how much time you want to spend apologizing to and begging help from other employees when they call out or drop the ball yet again.

The negative impact of unreliability can be particularly insidious in professions where employees have a client base (e.g., accountants, lawyers, consultants, etc.), as reliable employees will need to accrue client-specific knowledge *before* they can begin helping unreliable colleagues with their tasks. For example, a recently hired accountant at a midsize firm revealed they had missed several third-quarter client deadlines and insinuated they might need more time off to celebrate the holidays properly. The manager who reached out to the other accountants, asking them to learn the new hire's clients well enough to complete the monthly and year-end closing entries accurately on top of their own client loads, was not met with festive cheer.

Job Readiness

Ability to reliably perform tasks at a minimum level of competence is obviously important in a new hire. If your employees are overworked, some help may be better than no help—assuming the new hire requires minimal training. Keep in mind that training is expensive and time-consuming. Positions that require high levels of on-the-job training burden other employees, who spend time and energy helping newcomers learn and fixing their mistakes.

Beyond the task-specific skills, look for candidates with a growth mindset. People with this mindset believe knowledge and abilities can be developed with effort. This trait can be assessed with survey items or interview questions—for example, "Describe a situation when you did not perform well. If you faced that situation again tomorrow, what would you do differently?"[4]

Positive Attitude

Like germs, emotions are contagious.[5] One negative individual can "infect" others, bringing the whole team down and making the already challenging workload even harder.

Many employees will go as far as to actually change their task workflow to avoid someone they don't like, which creates all sorts of additional coordination costs, reductions in backup behavior, and decreases in extra-role behaviors.[6] Suddenly your employees who were happy to serve on that extra committee or help to keep the break room tidy are too busy or just happened to bring in a personal coffee machine for their office. If employees cease doing discretionary tasks, it has a cascading effect on other employees, who end up accomplishing less work and becoming more dissatisfied in the process.

Good Communication

Being able to communicate well with colleagues is important in any work environment, but working in virtual teams heightens the importance of frequent communication and trust and amplifies the potential impact of a negative team member. The separation between team members makes it easier to "hide" and harder to "seek"—it's much easier to ignore an email than someone standing at your office door. And for projects that require professionals with different areas of expertise—such as engineers, scientists, or design thinkers—to work together virtually, an ornery individual can derail the whole team.

Managers can assess basic communication skills during an interview by looking for a variety of factors, including the clarity and coherence of responses.[7] Also consider asking the candidate about their preferred communication medium and favorite tips/tricks for being an effective communicator. If the potential hire for your virtual team hates email and their big tip is never to call after 4:30 p.m., you may wish to keep looking.

How to Support an Understaffed Team

So, you don't have any qualified candidates right now. What can you do in the meantime? First, communicate to your employees that the challenge is temporary and that you're trying to hire good coworkers for them. Many employees would prefer to work a little extra for several weeks rather than deal with a bad hire long term. You may also consider asking your employees to help you recruit with an employee referral program.[8]

It's also critical to attend to your employees who choose to stay. Consider strategies to manage burnout and boost retention. Your current employees need respect, attention, rewards, and engagement. With increasing numbers of jobs offering hefty signing bonuses, it's important to try to make sure the grass isn't greener on the other side.[9]

If it might take a while to find the right "somebody," consider whether you should hire for a different position to take some of the pressure off your team. For example, perhaps you can't find a qualified sous chef—could you hire another line cook, dishwasher, or expediter? Hiring support staff is a common practice in health care (e.g., hiring medical scribes to support physicians) and higher education (e.g., hiring teaching assistants to support professors) and may need to increase in the future. Knowledge workers can increase their productivity by 20% by dropping or delegating lower-value tasks to someone else.

In addition, now is a great time to consider whether the right somebody needs to actually *be* a somebody. Beyond the use of robots in warehouses, factories, and restaurants, advancements in artificial intelligence have enabled new forms of collaboration between machines and knowledge workers.

If you don't have any applicants who are likely to be reliable and possess a growth mindset, positive attitude, and decent communication skills, hiring nobody is probably preferable to hiring somebody—at least in the short term. In the meantime, consider how you can support your current employees and whether filling a different position may be a better approach.

—————————

Margaret M. Luciano is an associate professor of management and organization in the Smeal College of Business at Pennsylvania State University.

Maximilian K. Watson is a PhD student of management and organization in the Smeal College of Business at Pennsylvania State University.

NOTES

1. Anne D'Innocenzio, "Companies Loosen Job Requirements but Challenges Remain," AP News, September 3, 2021, https://apnews .com/article/business-26fde6047db0827fd108dd7ce7ec673a.

2. "What Is a 3-2-2 Workweek?," City Personnel, March 31, 2021, https://citypersonnel.net/what-is-a-3-2-2-workweek/.

3. Lin Grensing-Pophal, "Creative and Compliant Ways to Check References," SHRM, May 8, 2019, https://www.shrm.org/topics-tools/ news/talent-acquisition/creative-compliant-ways-to-check-references.

4. "Growth Mindset Scale," Stanford|SPARQtools, https://sparqtools.org/mobility-measure/growth-mindset-scale/ #all-survey-questions.

5. Crystal Raypole, "Emotional Contagion: Why Emotions Are Contagious," Healthline, December 12, 2019, https://www.healthline .com/health/emotional-contagion.

6. Semin Park, John E. Mathieu, and Travis J. Grosser, "A Network Conceptualization of Team Conflict," *Academy of Management Review* 45 (2020): 352–375, https://doi.org/10.5465/amr.2016.0472.

7. "Want To Learn About a Candidate's Communication Skills? Ask These Interview Questions," Forbes Communications Council, Forbes, February 23, 2018; updated March 2, 2018, https://www.forbes .com/sites/forbescommunicationscouncil/2018/02/23/want-to-learn -about-a-candidates-communication-skills-ask-these-interview -questions/?sh=1d68c81d120c; Jamie Birt, "Communication Skills Interview Questions with Example Answers," Indeed, March 10, 2023, https://www.indeed.com/career-advice/interviewing/communication -interview-questions.

8. Roy Maurer, "Employee Referrals Remain Top Source for Hires," SHRM, June 23, 2017, https://www.shrm.org/topics-tools/ news/talent-acquisition/employee-referrals-remain-top-source-hires.

9. Patrick Thomas, "This Summer, Jobs Come with a Hefty Signing Bonus," *Wall Street Journal*, July 1, 2021, https://www.wsj.com/articles/ for-many-jobs-signing-bonuses-of-1-000and-upare-the-new-norm -11625131800.

Index

Index

Smart advice and inspiration from a source you trust.

If you enjoyed this book and want more comprehensive guidance on essential professional skills, turn to the HBR Guides Boxed Set. Packed with the practical advice you need to succeed, this seven-volume collection provides smart answers to your most pressing work challenges, from writing more effective emails and delivering persuasive presentations to setting priorities and managing up and across.

Harvard Business Review Guides

Available in paperback or ebook format. Plus, find downloadable tools and templates to help you get started.

Better Business Writing
Building Your Business Case
Buying a Small Business
Coaching Employees
Delivering Effective Feedback
Finance Basics for Managers
Getting the Mentoring You Need
Getting the Right Work Done

- Leading Teams
- Making Every Meeting Matter
- Managing Stress at Work
- Managing Up and Across
- Negotiating
- Office Politics
- Persuasive Presentations
- Project Management

HBR.ORG/GUIDES

Buy for your team, clients, or event.
Visit hbr.org/bulksales for quantity discount rates.

Notes

Notes

Notes

Notes

Notes

Notes

Notes

Notes

Notes

Notes

Notes